OCCASIONAL PUBLICATION NO. 21

Charles Ackers' Ornament Usage

BY

J. C. ROSS

Oxford Bibliographical Society
Bodleian Library
Oxford
1990

ISBN 0 901420 45 X

Printed in Great Britain at The Alden Press, Oxford

Contents

Acknowledgements

THIS work embodies the contributions of many people, and could not have been carried through without their help generously given.

I am beyond measure grateful to Professor Donald F. McKenzie (now Reader in Textual Criticism at the University of Oxford), who has answered innumerable enquiries with wonderful grace and thoroughness. Mr Paul Morgan of the Bodleian Library, and Mrs Diana Gurney of Camden Town, London, have also been most generous with their time and expertise, in examining books in response to enquiries from New Zealand.

Many librarians in several countries have dealt with specific queries with great kindness, and in some cases facilitated the supply of photocopies, microfilms or prints. They include: Mr John Bidwell, of the William Andrews Clark Memorial Library, University of California at Los Angeles; Miss Lilian A. Clark of the Cornell University Libraries; Mrs M. Czigány of University College Library, University of London; Ms Sheila Edward of the Bodleian Library; Ms Beverley Felman of Harvard College Library, and Ms Patrice Moskow of the Monroe C. Gutman Library, at Harvard; Mr Stephen Ferguson of Princeton University Library; Mr James Gilreath of the Library of Congress; Mr Richard Goulden and Mr D. D. Pereira of the British Library; Ms Dianne M. Gutscher of Bowdoin College Library; Ms Eleanor Hamlyn of Auckland Public Library; Mrs Patricia M. Howell of the Beinecke Rare Book and Manuscript Library, Yale University; Miss Cathie Hutchinson of Auckland University Library; Mr W. S. Hutton of Pembroke College Library, Cambridge; Ms Jennifer B. Lee of Brown University, Providence, Rhode Island; Mme. Andrée Lheritier and M. Claude Phillipon of the Bibliothèque Nationale, Paris; Ms Miriam Mandelbaum of the New York Public Library; Mr John Morris of the National Library of Scotland; Mr Alan E. Morrison of the Fine Arts Library, University of Pennsylvania; Mr Richard W. Ryan of the William L. Clements Library, University of Michigan; Mr N. Frederick Nash of the University of Illinois Library; Mr M. J. Phillips of the University of Keele Library; Ms Irene Pollock and Mr M. V. Roberts of the Guildhall Library, London; Mr Edwin Spragg of the Albert R. Mann Library, New York State Colleges, at Cornell University; and Mr Sem C. Sutter and Miss Clarice M. Zdanski of the Joseph Regenstein Library, University of Chicago.

More generally, I am grateful to the librarians of the British Library, of the Bodleian Library, of the Rare Books Room of the Cambridge University Library, and of the Alexander Turnbull Library, National Library of New Zealand.

I also appreciate the information and advice given by Professor Wallace Kirsop of Monash University, Mr James Mitchell of the Lincoln Institute, University of

Melbourne, Dr Peter Wallis of Newcastle upon Tyne, and Mr Keith Maslen of the University of Otago. My colleagues Dr William Broughton and Dr John Dawick at Massey University have read my Introduction at various stages of composition and given helpful advice.

Searches of the Eighteenth Century Short Title Catalogue file for Ackers and Palmer imprints, carried out by Blaise, the British Library Automated Information Service, have been of great value in identifying previously untraced items.

I am grateful to the Oxford Bibliographical Society for its willingness to publish this study, and to Professor John Feather and Dr H. R. Woudhuysen, the Society's President and editor, for their help and advice. I am deeply grateful for the expert editorial contribution of Dr Woudhuysen, whose eagle eye and more recent access to the primary material saved me from perpetuating a considerable number of errors.

I thank the Humanities and Social Science Research Fund Committee of Massey University for two financial grants to help with the purchase of photocopies and photographs, and thank the Vice-Chancellor of Massey for the grant of sabbatical study leave.

Finally, I acknowledge with gratitude the contribution of my wife Audrey, whose support and encouragement have been essential to the completion of this study.

J. C. Ross

Massey University
Palmerston North
New Zealand

Sources of Reproductions

THE majority of the ornaments, all those not otherwise specified, have been reproduced by permission of the Bodleian Library, Oxford.

Nos. 12, 13*, 37*, 39*, 44, 45, 46*, 50, 62*, 76, 80*, 81, 202 and 206* are reproduced by permission of the British Library.

Nos. 2*, 48, 113*, 114, 125, 171* and 204* are reproduced by permission of the Syndics of the University of Cambridge.

Nos. 60*, 181, 182*, 189*, 192*, 195*, 196* and 200* are reproduced by permission of the Library of Yale University.

Nos. 95* and 121* are reproduced by permission of the Rare Books and Manuscripts Division, the New York Public Library; Astor, Lennox and Tilden Foundations.

No. 42 is reproduced by permission of the Library of University College London.

No. 115 is reproduced by permission of the Harvard Graduate School of Education.

No. 193 is reproduced by permission of the Bibliothèque Nationale, Paris.

No. 208 is reproduced by permission of the Department of Special Collections, University of Chicago Library.

All ornaments have been reproduced approximately actual size. Where ornaments have had to be reduced in size, the degree of reduction has been noted in decimal form (in brackets).

Abbreviations

(*b*) *Other Abbreviations*

A1 (etc.)	A1 recto
A1^v (etc.)	A1 verso
Bowyer	Bowyer ornament, as in K. I. D. Maslen, *The Bowyer ornament stock*, O.B.S. occasional publication no. 8 (Oxford, 1973)
CA	Charles Ackers
ed.	edition (or, edited by)
Foxon	D. F. Foxon, *English verse 1701–1750*, 2 vols. (Cambridge, 1975)
Foxon, Review	—— review of *A ledger of Charles Ackers*, etc., in *The library*, 5th ser., 25 (1970), 65–73
Ledger	Charles Ackers' MS ledger as represented within the *Ledger*
Ledger	*A ledger of Charles Ackers printer of the London magazine*, ed. D. F. McKenzie and J. C. Ross, O.B.S. publications n.s. xv (Oxford, 1968)
LM	*London magazine*
McLaverty	J. McLaverty, *Pope's printer, John Wright: a preliminary study*, O.B.S. occasional publication no. 11 (Oxford, 1976)
N & Q	*Notes and queries*
O.B.S.	Oxford Bibliographical Society
orn(s)	ornament(s)
Post-CA	after Ackers' death, June 1759
prelims.	preliminaries
Pt.	Part
Richardson	Richardson ornament, as in William M. Sale, Jr., *Samuel Richardson: master printer*, Cornell studies in English no. 37 (Ithaca, NY, 1950)
Sale	as above
SP	Samuel Palmer
t.p.	title-page
vol(s)	volume(s)
Wallis	Peter J. and Ruth Wallis, *Biobibliography of British mathematics, part 2: 1701–1760* (Letchworth, 1986)
Woodfall	Henry Woodfall ornament, as in Richard J. Goulden, *The ornament stock of Henry Woodfall 1719–1747*, occasional papers of the Bibliographical Society no. 3 (London, 1988)
Wright	Wright ornament, as in McLaverty above

SECTION I

Introduction

THIS study is designed to stand beside other records of the ornament usages of English printers of the hand-press period, following most nearly K. I. D. Maslen's account of *The Bowyer ornament stock* (1973).[1] It is concerned with relief cuts, of wood or metal, used for decorative purposes, and excludes both those used for illustration and arrays of cast type-ornaments. Included in separate subsections are four devices, that have an indexical (mainly identifying) function, and three engravings that are used as ornaments in conjunction with letterpress. These engravings would have been printed at the rolling press in separate premises. Nonetheless they would have been part of the intended ornamentation of the books concerned and so, in a sense, integrally related to those directly made use of by the printer.

Ackers' career, books and stock

Charles Ackers (1702?–1759) was a successful if not outstandingly prestigious or prosperous London printer, who is of particular interest as the printer and part-owner of the *London magazine*. The survival of one of his customer account ledgers has made it possible to document his output for roughly half of his career. This manuscript (henceforth referred to as the 'Ledger') has been edited for the Oxford Bibliographical Society by Professor Donald F. McKenzie and myself.[2]

Ackers completed his apprenticeship to Samuel Palmer on 6 July 1725, and remained in Palmer's employ until he set up as a master himself in late 1727. This relationship continued to be important to him even after Palmer died on 9 May 1732; in 1739 he took on Palmer's son as an apprentice for a minimal fee. The premises in

---

[1] K. I. D. Maslen, *The Bowyer ornament stock*, O.B.S. occasional publication no. 8 (Oxford, 1973). Other relevant studies are: William M. Sale, Jr., *Samuel Richardson: master printer*, Cornell studies in English no. 37 (Ithaca, NY, 1950); J. McLaverty, *Pope's printer, John Wright: a preliminary study*, O.B.S. occasional publication no. 11 (Oxford, 1976); and Richard Goulden, *The ornament stock of Henry Woodfall 1719–1747*, occasional papers of the Bibliographical Society no. 3 (London, 1988).

[2] *A ledger of Charles Ackers printer of The London Magazine*, ed. D. F. McKenzie and J. C. Ross, O.B.S. publications, n.s. xv (Oxford, 1968). An autograph letter from Ackers to the Reverend Thomas Birch, dated 3 June 1734, is in the British Library, MS Add. 4300, f.7. It reads:

Sir,

  Mr Cox desires you would call upon him the next time you go towards the Exchange.

    I am, sir, Your humble servt.

      Charles Ackers

Great Swan Alley, off St. John's Street, Clerkenwell, in which he set up his printing house, were presumably those which Palmer had occupied between 1718 and 1724, before shifting to the Lady Chapel of St. Bartholomew's the Great. At least 62 ornaments, more than one quarter of his stock, came to him from Palmer.

His career may be divided into three periods: pre-Ledger, from late 1727 to 1731; the Ledger years, from 1732 to 1747; and post-Ledger, from 1748 until his death in June 1759. In practice, things were less tidy. It seems likely that he phased in the use of the extant Ledger in late 1731 at about the time that arrangements were being made for launching the *London magazine* (its first issue was dated April 1732); and that he adopted a new one in early 1748 when he took his son John into partnership. The third period was punctuated by John's death on 21 April 1756, which defeated whatever hopes he had of perpetuating his business within his own family. It would seem that what survived of it was taken over by Henry Baldwin.

Our knowledge of the output of his printing house and, consequently, of his ornament-usage, even for the second period, inevitably remains incomplete. Of the 314 bookwork items mentioned in the Ledger with imprints dated 1732–47 (including also 3 for 1748), copies of 245 have been seen or reported on, but none have been located for 68 of the remaining 69.[3] Of these, 27 are further editions of Thomas Dyche's *A guide to the English tongue* and 10 are annual editions of *Goldsmith's almanac*.

Moreover, the Ledger itself is incomplete in its coverage. Several leaves have been torn out (two from the front, and two preceding and three following the last leaves bearing entries); and it is clear that certain activities, such as the printing of the *Weekly register* between 1730 and 1735, were not covered by it. An additional 21 items with 1732–47 imprints have been identified, 16 of them for 1732–33 and one each for 1734, 1735, 1736, 1746, and 1747. Whether *Mosis Chorenensis historiae Armeniacae* (1736) was dealt with on the missing first two leaves one cannot tell. It is a substantial scholarly work requiring the composition of parallel texts in Latin and in Armenian script; the processes of printing and of organising its publication by subscription would have stretched over a number of years, very possibly pre-dating the opening of the extant Ledger. It may well be that the previous ledger continued to be used until the customer accounts open in early 1732 were closed. In any event, it seems that the extant Ledger provides a wholly complete record of Ackers' printing activities only for the years 1737 to 1745.

The presence of his name in the imprint, or of ornaments known to have been in his stock, has made it possible to identify 127 books from the pre- and post-Ledger phases. Undoubtedly others remain to be found, especially for the third period. The evidence of ornaments needs to be used with caution. It is sometimes possible that printing was shared with one or more other printer(s). An ornament later known to have been in Ackers' stock may have been in use by him or by a previous owner. An ornament

---

[3] A copy of item 105, the 25th edition of Dyche's *Guide to the English tongue* (1738), has been located by Dr R. C. Alston in the collection of Professor Gabrielson in Stockholm, but has not been seen nor a report obtained (see *Ledger* entry).

perhaps previously borrowed by him may have been returned to its true owner (e.g., Palmer). A special case is presented by the first volume of Pyle's *Paraphrase on the Acts*, 4th edition (1750), in which three known Ackers ornaments are outnumbered by eight others. This is dealt with in Appendix III.

It follows then that our knowledge of the ornaments used by him is both incomplete and slightly hazy around the edges, giving the present study the status of a report on work in progress. Accordingly, the 40 ornaments observed in use once only have been numbered with an asterisk, to identify those about which the possibilities of borrowing, or of insecure attribution, might be considered.

Of 266 Ledger period items inspected (including the 3 listed items for 1748), 146 contain ornaments, and 113 of the 127 identified non-Ledger items also do so, amounting to 259 items containing a total of 211 ornaments (i.e., 134 items contain none). For these cuts, a significant degree of doubt as to whether Ackers printed the part of the book containing them extends (at most) to only 5, and the number likely to have been borrowed to about 12. The figure of 211 includes the 3 engravings, which would not have been part of the stock.

Concepts

Indeed, this study is concerned with 'usage' rather than 'stock'. In the case of Ackers, at least, the concept of 'usage' is more appropriate, being more comprehensive and precise, than that of 'stock', which implies ownership or at least custody of ornament-blocks over a finite period.[4] First, it allows for the possibility that ornaments observed in use once only may have been borrowed. Secondly, the dates of first and last observed use can be directly stated, whereas these may offer only a rough guide to the terminal dates between which an ornament was physically present in the stock. While the term 'stock' will continue to be employed in some contexts, it remains true that direct evidence is available only for 'usage', and that the make-up of the 'stock' is inferred from this, and may not wholly overlap with it.

The term 'item' is used here to denote a book or some other substantial piece of printing (as opposed to jobbing), such as has been given a separate numbered entry in Appendix I of the published *Ledger*. This practice accords separate identity to shared printing jobs but not to recognized re-issues. Moreover, as in the *Ledger* edition, the *London magazine* is given item-numbers in relation to its annual volumes, rather than to its monthly issues, and the whole six-year run of the *Weekly register* is considered a single 'item' (an exception is made in Table II, in which it is necessary to include it for each year of publication). Accordingly the actual number of separate units of printing would have been very much larger than these figures indicate.

In a similar way, in the discussion that follows, one 'use' of an ornament denotes its

---

[4] For printers like the Bowyers or John Watts, the broad identity of usage with stock may have been complete, in that they never borrowed ornaments. However, the respective terminal dates for use and ownership could have differed substantially.

appearance within one 'item', irrespective of how many times it appears within that item. Hence the number of 'uses' cited will in some cases correspond to the number of actual appearances, and in others be very much less (for example, the factotums 168, 198 and 203 appeared in the issues of the *London magazine* sometimes up to 12 times a year).

First use and frequency of use

In the following table the earliest appearances of ornaments are divided within periods; for the first two, the number in brackets is the number of ornaments which appear solely within this period. ('Medium' headpieces are here considered as those with a depth between 29.5 and 15 mm, 'medium' tailpieces those with a depth between 39.5 and 20 mm.)

TABLE I: *First Appearance of Ornaments by Period*

	1727–31	1732–47	1748–59	Sub-Totals	Totals
Headpieces:					
Large	2	9(5)	5	16	
Medium	9(2)	20(3)	5	34	
Thin	5	22(6)	4	31	81
Tailpieces:					
Large	5	9(3)	0	14	
Medium	6(1)	14(6)	1	21	
Small	2	5(2)	0	7	42
Initials	6	23(5)	1		30
Factotums	14(2)	30(14)	7		51
Devices	1	1	2		4
Engraved Orns.	1	2	0		3
Totals	51(5)	135(44)	25		211

As one might expect, first appearances of ornaments are quite numerous in the first and second periods, and much less common in the third; though this scarcity also reflects the relatively small number of items so far identified for this period (74 over 12 years; see Table II). What the table primarily reveals about Ackers' overall usage is the relatively large number of headpieces employed. On the other hand, 5 of the 16 large headpieces are the 'view of London' cuts used exclusively for the *London magazine*, that is, for the monthly title-pages from March 1746, and for the head of January issues from 1743 onwards (these might perhaps have been categorized as devices).[5] If these

___

[5] They simultaneously decorate and identify. Similarly no. 167, the factotum used for one observed advertisement for cockfighting in the *Weekly register*, might have been categorized functionally as a device, but has

were set aside, then the number of large headpieces is reduced to 11. As will be seen from Table III, 9 of these were used 4 times or less; and these uses occurred mainly before 1735. The limited use that is made of large blocks reflects the pattern of Ackers'

TABLE II: *Usage in each Year*

Year	Items Seen	New Orns.	Observed in Use	Cumul. Total
1727	1	2(2)	2	2
1728	16	17(13)	19	19
1729	16	19(7)	38	38
1730	11	3	37	41
1731	13	9	44	49
1732	21	24(7)	68	73
1733	18	24(11)	90	98
1734	17	26(9)	116	124
1735	19	14(5)	124	138
1736	13	0	119	138
1737	19	4(2)	122	142
1738	13	0	121	142
1739	18	3	122	145
1740	16	1	122	146
1741	16	0	120	146
1742	24	16(1)	135	162
1743	19	4(1)	126	166
1744	10	3	124	169
1745	12	1	124	170
1746	12	11	133	181
1747	11	2(1)	125	183
1748	7	5(1)	123	188
1749	8	1	117	189
1750	13	5(2)	115	194
1751	7	1	98	195
1752	5	4	96	199
1753	5	2	94	201
1754	9	4	93	205
1755	5	2	75	207
1756	4	1	62	207
1757	3	1	49	208
1758	3	0	48	208
1759	5	0	42	208

been retained within the main sequence for the sake of convenience. Three other minor devices seen in use in this journal in 1730–32 have been omitted: a small ship used above the shipping news from the issue of 12 December 1730 onwards, a small house occasionally used in 1731, with advertisements of properties for rent, and an advertising block of the 'Three Kings and Half Moon' used in July 1730 issues, which is also in the *Daily post-boy* of 25 August 1730, etc.

output.[6] Secondly, there are a relatively small number of ornamental initials and a large number of factotums. This is made clear by comparison with K. I. D. Maslen's reconstruction of the Bowyer stock, as the most complete record yet available for this time. Whereas the Bowyers over nearly 75 years used 86 initials belonging to 3 series, and 47 factotums, Ackers over nearly 32 years used 30 initials belonging to at least 13 series, and 51 factotums. It is likely that he acquired his initials secondhand in a piecemeal way, and never owned a full alphabet in any one series.

Table II shows how Ackers' known usage built up, and then during the third, post-Ledger period diminished. The figures for 'Items Seen' include the annual volumes of the *London magazine* and *Weekly register*. In cases where the Ledger account date is for a year earlier than that in the imprint, the former is used. In the 'New Ornaments' column the numbers in brackets indicate how many of the total given came to Ackers from Palmer. The figures for 'Observed in Use' are arrived at by adding new ornaments and deducting those last observed in use in the previous year. For this table, the 3 engravings are omitted, giving a total of 208 ornaments.

Obviously, the relatively small numbers of 'Items Seen' for most of the pre- and post-Ledger years once again affect the figures for 'New Ornaments' and for ornaments 'Observed in Use'. Nonetheless in examining many books printed in the 1750s one can observe a general tendency for the use of printers' ornaments to diminish, and a corresponding increase to occur in the use of fleurons (especially in the style of Fournier), though many English printers came to base the visual appeal of their books on elegant typography alone, with no decoration. Assuming Ackers was following this trend, one would expect that the true number of ornaments first brought into use by him during the 1750s would not have been much larger. Otherwise less use would have been made, in 1754 especially, of headpieces that were broken or badly worn. Indeed the 'Observed in Use' figures for the last few years may be too high, since they take account of ornaments in the 1759 edition of Price's *British carpenter*, which may well have been a re-issue of the 1753 edition.

Table III examines the approximate frequency with which ornaments have been observed in use throughout the whole of Ackers' career. The figures given indicate the number of ornaments in each category that occur a certain number of times; e.g., in the first line they indicate that four large headpieces (plus one engraved headpiece) occur once, and two between 15 and 19 times. Here the factotums also are divided into large, medium (from 29.5 to 20 mm in height), and small. In a divergence from previous practice, in the first line the four *London magazine* 'view of London' headpieces, nos. 1, 4, 5, and 6, are plotted in terms of their 'actual' number of uses, i.e., for monthly issues rather than for annual volumes, with the figures placed within square brackets (the monthly uses being $22 \times$, $36 \times$, $53 \times$, and $54 \times$, respectively). The engravings are noted in round brackets.

---

[6] The 356 items for which the format is known divide into: 2°—5.9% (21 items); 4°—8.7% (31); 8°—67.1% (239); 12°—13.5% (48); other ($1/2^\circ$, 16°, 24°)—4.8% (17). Of the 2° items, 14 represent shared printing.

TABLE III: *Frequency of Usage*

Approx. uses	1	2	3–4	5–9	10–14	15–19	20–24	25–29	30–34	35+
Hps: large	4(+1)	1	4	—	1(+1)	2	[1]	—	—	[3]
medium	7	2	4	8	6	2	3	2	1	—
thin	3	3	3	8	7	3	3	1	—	—
Tps: large	2	(1)	2	1	3	2	3	—	—	1
medium	2	2	2	6	1	4	2	—	1	1
small	1	—	—	3	1	1	—	1	—	—
Initials	4	5	6	3	4	4	2	1	—	1
Fms: large	—	—	—	2	1	1	—	—	—	—
medium	2	—	—	4	1	6	1	—	—	1
small	13	3	1	2	2	6	1	1	1	1
Devices	2	2	—	—	—	—	—	—	—	—
Totals	40(+1)	18(+1)	22	37	27(+1)	31	16	6	3	8

What these figures conceal is, especially, the very large number of uses of factotums in the successive issues of the *London magazine*. On the other hand it is surprising to find such a large number of small factotums used once only (i.e., within a single item). The majority of large headpieces appear very few times, and as noticed above, mainly before 1735.

Nature of output and stock

The character and quality of Ackers' ornament stock can be related to the nature of his business. In the first few years he printed quite a few elegantly produced items, including such literary works as the poetry of James Ralph, using high quality cuts mostly in good condition.[7] However, the booksellers he dealt with were mainly concerned with steadier-selling, more pedestrian fare. By the mid-1740s a pattern was clearly set; in terms of sheets printed, the *London magazine* represented about a quarter of the output of his shop, and new editions of a dozen frequently reprinted works made up another half: school textbooks, dictionaries, Richard Hayes' *Interest at one view*, and the *Whole book of psalms*, *Goldsmith's almanac* and one sheet of *Poor Robin's almanac*, the last three for the Stationers' Company's English Stock. (In terms of quantity of composition, the *London magazine* with its relatively small type and compact setting would have constituted a significantly higher proportion of the work done.) Most of the bookwork within the remaining quarter was similar in kind: respectable, but only occasionally making much claim to prestige, whether for the

[7] Professor Pat Rogers mentions Ackers as 'a printer of more than one duncely production', in *Grub Street: studies in a subculture* (London, 1969), p. 159. These would include works by Ralph, Boyer, Oldmixon and Musgrave.

quality of the content, or for the printing. There were a few exceptions, such as John Warburton's *London and Middlesex illustrated* and *Vallum romanum*, and Francis Price's books, which could rank as 'fine printing', though not of the highest order. Work from his shop was always tidily and competently printed; but the ambition one may guess at from the evidence of some of his earliest books to match Palmer's best work was rarely fulfilled.

As a corollary, while most of his ornaments were respectable, they ranged from very high quality to just middling. Some of the high quality cuts were already imperfect when he first used them, and he continued to do so long after they developed further defects and wear. Nearly half his stock (93 cuts) were demonstrably acquired secondhand. A few blocks, acquired perhaps in job-lots, and tried out once in relatively unimportant books, were already badly worn. By comparison with the Bowyer or Woodfall stocks, much of Ackers' collection is somewhat more modest, either in quality or in condition, and reflects the 'middle to upper-middle' area of the market which he occupied. Nonetheless it may be observed that in selecting exemplars of impressions to be photographed for Section II, it has not always been practical to pick the earliest or best uses.

Provenance

The surviving Ledger provides no information about the acquisition, borrowing or sale of ornaments; hence, dating can be provided only for earliest and latest observed uses. At least 83 of them came to him secondhand from other known printers: 62 from Samuel Palmer, some indirectly, 8 (or 9) from Robert Walker, 6 (or 5) from William (and/or E.) Rayner, 2 each from James Roberts and Edward Say, and 1 each from John Huggonson (not a Palmer block), James Redmayne and 'J.P.' (John Purser?). Ten are from unidentified printers. These are listed in Section IV (3). Some others also appear to have not been new when Ackers first used them.

The value for Ackers of his relationship with his previous master, Samuel Palmer, has already been mentioned. One hundred and thirty-eight items printed by Palmer have so far been identified, which will represent only a fraction of his output (see Appendix II). Further study would undoubtedly reveal even more ornaments passing from Palmer to Ackers. It may be that between late 1727 and May 1732 a certain degree of sharing took place, with certain ornaments that appeared in Ackers' books being borrowed, and only at some later time added to his stock. On the other hand, quite a few were never used by Ackers. Some of these have been observed in books printed by John Huggonson, Palmer's partner between 1729 and 1732. At least 11 came to Ackers through Huggonson.

Judging from their first appearances, listed in Table II above, and Section IV, Palmer's ornaments were evidently acquired in several batches. Their first observed uses were: 2 (1727), 13 (1728), 7 (1729), 7 (1732), 11 (1733), 9 (1734), 5 (1735), 2 (1737), 1 (1742, 1743, 1747, 1748), and 2 (1750). Nonetheless some of these could have been in

Ackers' possession for several years before they were first made use of; for example, the ornamental initials B and G (nos. 132★ and 135), first observed in use in 1750 and 1747 respectively, are among the less satisfactorily designed members of a set of initials of which he used two in 1729 and another four in 1733. Quite a few of the ornaments appearing in 1728 and 1729 were already slightly damaged, and may have been given or sold to Ackers for this reason. In two known cases (nos. 127 and 128) Palmer retained variants in superior condition.

The proportion of identified ex-Palmer ornaments, constituting more than a quarter of Ackers' stock, does not sufficiently indicate their full importance. They include 4 of the 10 headpieces used more than 19 times, and 6 of the 19 used between 10 and 19 times (apart from those used specifically for the *London magazine*), as well as virtually all the larger tailpieces.

One gains an impression of Ackers as an anxious squirrel, who retained a special fondness for his old master's ornaments. For whatever reason, even of the small group of blocks first observed in use in the 1750s, most were manifestly secondhand. It may be that good cuts in the richly detailed 'Hoffmanesque' style that he liked were obtainable in no other way. That he continued, in that decade, to use blocks that had been cut in the 1720s, or earlier, gave some of his books a distinctly conservative appearance.

Borrowing, lending, and later use

While firm conclusions cannot be built on negative and incomplete evidence, a single observed use relatively early in a printer's career suggests an ornament was borrowed rather than bought. This consideration applies for headpieces 2★ (1734), 15★ (1740), 24★ and 34★ (both 1729) and 40★ (1734); tailpieces 93★ (1735), 104★ (1729) and 113★ (1734); the initial 147★ (1729); the factotums 167 (1730) (see note 5 above) and 171★ (1730); and the royal arms 205★ (1745). No. 15★ was borrowed, probably from James Roberts, for use in the second edition of Asplin's *Alkibla*, Part I (1740), because of its illustrative relevance to 'worshipping towards the east'. At least one of the four ornaments used in 1728 and 1729 in Ralph's poems was borrowed from Palmer. No. 93★ seems to have been borrowed rather than bought from John Huggonson for use in Tatersal's *The bricklayer's miscellany* in 1735.

Conversely Huggonson made use of two of Ackers' blocks, nos. 72 and 177, for use in the *Memoirs of the society of Grub-street* (1737), Volume I, and probably borrowed no. 22 in 1733 for use in *Al Mesra* (1734 but advertised in *LM*, November 1733).

In 1758 six of Ackers' known ornaments, plus one other, were used in *A journal of the campaign on the coast of France*, 'Printed and sold by J. Townsend'. Townsend, the son of a 'merchant', had been bound as an apprentice by Ackers in 1750, and freed and clothed on 6 December 1757. He himself bound an apprentice on 7 December 1761.

After Ackers' death in June 1759 a few of his ornaments continued to be used in the *London magazine*, the last of them in 1764.

Cutters

Twenty of Ackers' blocks (10 headpieces, 4 tailpieces, 2 initials and 4 factotums) bear the initials 'FH', indicating they were cut by the prolific Francis Hoffman (fl. 1706–1725); and at least 20 others are close enough in style to be imitations of his designs. Three of the signed blocks (nos. 33, 87, and 104★) co-existed with close variants also signed 'FH' or 'F. Hoffman'. Of the 20, 6 were demonstrably acquired from Palmer, 4 from Robert Walker, and 2 from William and E. Rayner.[8]

The only other cutter of woodblocks whose work was signed was 'T. Davies', who provided the view-of-London headpieces used for the monthly title-pages of the *London magazine* from March 1746 onwards. Only three of the four used during Ackers' lifetime were signed, but the fourth of them, and also the smaller version, and the St. Paul's factotum (nos. 9 and 162), both of which appeared on the first page of the text of the January issues from 1743 onwards, are close enough in content and style to be almost certainly his work as well.

The *London magazine* headpieces

Between 1732 and February 1746 the *London magazine* had no monthly title-page, unlike its major competitor the *Gentleman's magazine* which had Cave's St. John's Gate device above a table of contents. Instead, the monthly issues evidently had a paper wrapper bearing a half-title, a list of contents, and advertisements (see Appendix I, item 270); and the annual title-page had as a vignette a view of the City of London (no. 209) engraved by John Pine. Until 1743 the headpieces on the first page of each issue were constructs of arabesque fleurons, either a series identifiable in Caslon's type-specimen of 1734, or else a group (deriving from Plantin or Granjon designs) that had been used in Palmer's proposals for his *General history of printing*, issued in 1729.[9]

In 1743 no. 9 was introduced for the January issue, and in 1744 no. 52 for the other monthly issues, although it split within the first two months of use. No. 51 first appeared in the February 1745 issue, and remained in use until as late as 1764; hence it may well have been a metal block.

From March 1746 onwards monthly title-pages came into use, with a large headpiece above a table of contents. The first version (no. 1), signed '*T Davies*' with a swash *D*, appears to have been made as part of an even larger block, which incorporated within its outer box-frame the view of London, the magazine's title

---

[8] 'FH' ornaments: nos. 11, 19, 20, 24★, 28, 29, 33, 36, 37★, 43, 87, 102, 104★, 118, 133★, 145, 159, 160, 161, 178. From Palmer: 29, 33, 87, 102, 145, 159. From Walker: 19, 28, 37★, 43, 161. From Rayner: 20, 36, 37★?. From Say: 178. Unidentified printer: 24★, 33, 104★. No previous observed use: 11, 118, 133★, 160.

[9] John Ryder, *Flowers and flourishes: including a newly annotated edition of A suite of fleurons* (London, 1976); within *A suite of fleurons*, pp. 27–31. A fine construct of fleurons is used as a headpiece in the first edition of James Ralph's poem *Night* (1728), one of Ackers' earliest books. An incomplete copy of Palmer's prospectus is in the British Library Ames. 6, as item 2742.

(within a box) and a factotum slot for the month and year. It became split vertically right of centre during its first use, for the March 1746 issue, and continued to appear in this condition until the end of the following year. The use it received was very heavy, 7000 copies of the magazine being printed each month. The unusually great depth and the slot may well have made it too vulnerable; or else the replacement cost of so large a block may have been deemed too high. At any rate, subsequent versions comprised the pictorial element only, and the other features were made up with type and with box-frames of rules. The second version (no. 5), signed 'T *Davies*' with a non-swash *D*, appeared from February 1748 to June 1752; the third (no. 6), unsigned and the poorest in quality, from July 1752 to December 1756; and the fourth (no. 4), signed 'TD', from January 1757 to the end of 1759, though it was already split by May 1757. These blocks were also damaged in other ways, and the publishers seem to have accepted that this was inevitable.

Their initial reluctance to follow Cave's example in using a monthly title-page may well have derived from their sensitivity to charges of plagiarizing his 'magazine' format, discussed in the *Ledger* introduction (pp. 5–8).

The view of London engraved by Pine resembled that which formed the central section of the headpiece for the *London journal* from 1719 to 1734; and this doubtless helped to stress the principle of continuity with the weekly journals on which the magazine based its claim to legitimacy in its long-running contest with its rival.

Arrangement of sections

Reproductions of all ornaments known to have been used by Ackers are provided in Section II. They have been divided into headpieces, tailpieces, initials, factotums, devices, and engravings used as ornaments, and within each category ranked in order of decreasing height and, where several have the same height, in order of decreasing width. Where two or more ornamental initials recognizably belong to the same series, they have been ranked in alphabetical order.

It should be appreciated that impressions made with the same block will differ slightly in size due to varying paper-movement, and to the progressive deterioration and trimming of much-used blocks over a period of time. All the same, given that the total number of ornaments here is not very large there is no risk of confusion in relying upon dimensions, taking as standard those of the exemplars reproduced.

James Mitchell of the University of Melbourne has recently advocated the classification of ornaments in terms of graphic subjects.[10] I have found some difficulty in seeking to apply it when the 'subject' is rather indeterminate, and when a design is complicated with minor pictorial elements. Nonetheless it may gain broader acceptance, and an attempt to apply it is included in Section IV (4).

[10] James Mitchell, 'The taxonomy of printers' ornaments', *Bibliographical society of Australia and New Zealand bulletin*, 9: 2 (1985), 54–60.

Section III provides notes about each of Ackers' known ornaments, as explained in its preamble; the data are analysed in several ways in Section IV.

Since the publication of the *Ledger* in 1968 a good deal of fresh information has come to light about Ackers' printing, and this is listed in Appendix I. The manifest importance of Samuel Palmer's printing in relation to the provenance of many of Ackers' ornaments has made necessary a preliminary check-list of Palmer's known books; this is given in Appendix II, as a forerunner to a more extensive study of Palmer's book production and ornament usage.

14 33 × 92

15★ 32 × 87

16 30 × 87

17 29.5 × 80

17

18 29 × 85

19 28 × 121

20 28 × 85

21 28 × 84

22 28 × 72

23 27 × 90 (0.93)

24★ 27 × 86 (0.93)

25 26.5 × 86.5 (0.92)

26 26.5 × 83 (0.92)

27 25.5 × 75 (0.93)

28 25 × 134

29 25 × 83

30★ 25 × 83

31 24 × 72.5 (0.94)

32 24 × 69 (0.93)

33 23.5 × 72 (0.94)

34★ 23 × 86 (0.93)

35 23 × 80 (0.92)

36 23 × 78.5 (0.93)

37★ 22 × 71 (0.93)

38 22 × 73 (0.92)

39★ 22 × 69 (0.94)

40★ 21 × 108

41 21 × 79 (0.92)

42 20 × 79 (0.92)

43 20 × 75   **44** 20 × 59

45 19 × 86 (0.93)   **46★** 19 × 72 (0.92)

47 19 × 68 (0.93)   **48** 18.5 × 85 (0.94)

49 18.5 × 77 (0.92)   **50** 18 × 73 (0.94)

51 13 × 100

22

52 12 × 101

53 12 × 88

54 12 × 83

55 11 × 103

56 11 × 85

57 11 × 77

58 11 × 71

59 10.5 × 81

60★ 10 × 90

61 10 × 85

62★ 10 × 79

63 10 × 72

64 9 × 104

65 9 × 86

66 9 × 85

67 8.5 × 83

68 8 × 72

69 7 × 70

70 6.5 × 76

71 6.5 × 75

72 6 × 77

73 6 × 77

74 6 × 76

75 5 × 83

76 5.5 × 66

77 5 × 87

78 5 × 81

79 5 × 80.5

80★ 5 × 78

81 5 × 60

82 58 × 63

83 57 × 72

84 52 × 76

85 52 × 64

86 51 × 62.5

87 46 × 55

88 46 × 53

89 45 × 61

90 45 × 60

91 45 × 52

92 43 × 56

93★ 43 × 64

94 42 × 64

95★ 40 × 66

96 39 × 52

97 37 × 58

98 37 × 39

99 36 × 59

100 34 × 65.5

101 34 × 31

102 33.5 × 50

103 31 × 44

104★ 29 × 46

105 29 × 33

106 28.5 × 41

107 28 × 42

108 25 × 55

109 25 × 37.5

110 25 × 37

111 25 × 32

112 24 × 44

113★ 24 × 31

114 23 × 23

115 22 × 34

116 20 × 27

117 19.5 × 36   **118** 19 × 26   **119** 15 × 29   **120** 14 × 41

121★ 10 × 29   **122** 10 × 22   **123** 9 × 47

INITIALS

124 37 × 37   **125** 37 × 37   **126** 37 × 37

127 33 × 32   **128** 34 × 32   **129** 34 × 32

130 31 × 31   **131** 31 × 32   **132**★ 28.5 × 25   **133**★ 28 × 25

134 29 × 25   **135** 29 × 26.5   **136** 26 × 23   **137** 27 × 23.5

138 29 × 25.5   **139** 29 × 27   **140** 28 × 25   **141** 28 × 25

142 25 × 25   **143** 24.5 × 26   **144** 23.5 × 24   **145** 22 × 22

32

146 20.5 × 20   **147★** 20 × 20   **148** 19 × 20   **149** 17 × 16.5

150★ 17 × 16   **151** 17 × 17   **152** 17 × 16.5   **153** 16 × 16

FACTOTUMS

154 36 × 35   **155** 34 × 31   **156** 32 × 29

157 31 × 31   **158** 29.5 × 23   **159** 29 × 29

33

160 29 × 27

161 27.5 × 28

162 27 × 25

163 27 × 25

164 26 × 24

165 25 × 24

166 24.5 × 24

167 20 × 23.5

168 20 × 20

169 20 × 20

170★ 20 × 19

171★ 20 × 19

172 20 × 18

173 20 × 18

174 19 × 19

175 19 × 19

176 19 × 18

177 18.5 × 16.5

178 18 × 18

179★ 18 × 17.5

180 18 × 17   **181** 18 × 17   **182★** 18 × 15   **183** 17.5 × 17.5   **184** 17.5 × 17.5

185 17.5 × 17   **186** 17 × 17   **187★** 17 × 16   **188★** 17 × 16   **189★** 17 × 16

190★ 17 × 16   **191★** 17 × 16   **192★** 17 × 16   **193** 16.5 × 17   **194** 16.5 × 17

195★ 16.5 × 16.5   **196★** 16.5 × 16   **197** 16.5 × 16   **198** 16 × 17   **199** 16 × 17

200★ 16 × 16   **201** 16 × 16   **202** 15 × 15   **203** 15 × 15   **204★** 13.5 × 13

DEVICES

205★ 59 × 84

206★ 48 × 64

207 47 × 42.5

208 35 × 50

ENGRAVINGS

209 66.5 × 107

210★ 34.5 × 71

211 60 × 118

SECTION III

Notes on Individual Ornaments

FOR each ornament the basic information listed is: dimensions (height × width) to the nearest half-millimetre; terminal dates of known use; number of known uses, as defined in Section I (for some *London magazine* headpieces, the number of monthly uses is given in brackets); and the source of the impression reproduced, with the pressmark of the copy. Further details may be given of: signing by a woodblock-cutter ('FH' is Francis Hoffman); condition, noting the development of significant damage; previous use by another printer ('SP' is Samuel Palmer, in effect between 1729 and 1732 the Palmer-Huggonson partnership), and/or in a particular book; and close variants, listed in terms of the printer concerned (where known), and/or of the book in which they have been observed. In a few cases data are given of use after Ackers' death ('Post-CA'). The short titles of books have been further shortened, where convenient and compatible with accuracy and correct identification. Palmer's books are referred to by author or key words of title, and date, related to the listing in Appendix II. The locations of ornaments within books in the 'Previous use' and 'Variant' statements are generally omitted when they are within the preliminaries or the first sheet of the text.

Headpieces

1 81 × 115; 1746–47; twice (22 ×). *LM*. March 1746. On π1 (monthly t.p.). O (Hope Adds. 401). Signed '*T Davies*'. Pictorial element 50 × 111, within (probably) integrated block with factotum slot. Condition: in some examples of first use, in March 1746, intact; in others, near-vertical split developed right of centre; by July, notch in frame, upper right.

2★ 54 × 155; 1734; once. Stackhouse, T. *A complete body of speculative and practical divinity*. 2nd ed. 1734. On a1. C (Huntingdon 24.1).

3 52 × 132; 1733–38; 3 ×. Price, F. *A treatise on carpentry*. 1733. On A2. O (Don. d. 191). Condition: by 1726, outer frame damaged, lower right. Previous use: SP, in Leybourn (1722) to Edwards (1726), Fleury (1727); Huggonson, in Pope, A., *Essay on man, First epistle*, 1st ed. (publ. Feb. 1733). (First used by Ackers in Price, publ. May.) Variant: Richardson 5 (rectangular).

4 51 × 111; 1757–59; 3 × (36 ×). *LM*. January 1757. On A1 (monthly t.p.). O (Hope Adds. 412). Signed 'TD'. Condition: by May 1757, split from left of centre down to centre; by November 1759, split from centre down to far right.

5 50 × 113; 1748–52; 5 × (53 ×). *LM.* February 1748. On G1 (monthly t.p.). O (Hope Adds. 403). Signed 'T *Davies*'. Condition: by February 1748, two blotches on St. Paul's west tower; by March 1752, central slanting split.

6 49 × 112; 1752–56; 5 × (54 ×). *LM.* July 1752. On 2P1 (monthly t.p.). O (Hope Adds. 407). Unsigned. Condition: from July 1752, vertical cut near right edge; by September 1754, near-vertical split left of centre.

7 40 × 159; 1729–34; twice. [Lonsdale, M.] *The loss of liberty.* 1729. On B1. O (Vet. A4 c. 24 (5)). Previous use: J. Roberts?, in [Badeslade, T.] *The history of the navigation . . . of the port of King's Lyn* [2nd ed.] (1726). Used in Stackhouse, T., *A complete body of divinity* (1729), on the contents leaf ★1 (in C copy), possibly contributed by Ackers.

8★ 40 × 134; 1753; once. Price, F. *A series of . . . observations upon the cathedral-church of Salisbury.* 1753. On A2. O (4° Godw. 10). Previous uses: in Young, E., *The instalment* (1726), and in Patrick, S., *Commentary upon the Old Testament* (1743), Vol. III.

9 40 × 104; 1743–59; 17 ×. *LM.* January 1743. On A1. O (Hope Adds. 398). Heads first page of text for January issues. Condition: by 1744, upper left side damaged, subsequently repaired; by 1752, trimmed at left edge; by 1757, split left of centre. Post-CA use: *LM*, 1760–62.

10 37 × 89; 1728–52; 3 ×. *LM.* 1737. On a2 (prelims.). O (Hope Adds. 392).

11 35 × 131; 1753–59; 4 ×. Price, F. *The British carpenter.* 3rd ed. 1753. On [A]2. O (GG 121 Art.). Signed 'FH'.

12 34 × 138; 1734–50; 4 ×. Price, F. *The British carpenter.* 2nd ed. 1735. On A3. L (7943.i.11). Condition: trimmed at left. Previous use: by W. Rayner, in *The miter* [n.d., *ca.*1730], printed for E. Rayner.

13★ 34 × 110; 1746; once. Hayes, R. *A new method for valuing of annuities upon lives.* 2nd ed. 1746. On B3. L (60.d.15).

14 33 × 92; 1746–58; 13 ×. *LM.* 1747. On π2 (annual prelims.). O (Hope Adds. 402). Condition: by 1757, right edge uneven.

15★ 32 × 87; 1740; once. [Asplin, W.] *Alkibla.* Pt. I. 2nd ed. 1740. On C1. O (137 e. 114). Previous use: J. Roberts?, in *Alkibla*, Pt. I, 1st ed. (1728); in Gibbs, P., *A letter to the congregation of protestant dissenters of Hackney*, 3rd ed. (1737). Borrowed?

16 30 × 87; 1733–55; 18 ×. Simpson, T. *Elements of plane geometry.* 1747. On A2. O (8° C 950 Linc.). Previous use: SP, in [Cooke, T.] *Comedian* (1732), IV; earlier, William and John Innys, in Ray, J., *The wisdom of God*, etc., 8th ed. (1722). Condition: nail risen to right of base of plinth (metal block); gash in inner frame, above, to right of head; by 1750, dent in inner frame, above, 7 mm from right corner. Variants: in Philips, A., *Humfrey, Duke of Gloucester, a tragedy* (1723) (better quality); in Love, J., and Ruddiman, T., *Two grammatical treatises* (Edinburgh, 1733).

17 29.5 × 80; 1734–59; 25 ×. Philipps, J. T. *Dissertationes historicae quatuor.* 1735. On A2. O (8° F 224 Linc.). Previous use: SP, in *Comedian* (1732), II; Huggonson, in *The life of Mr. Woolston* (1733).

18 29 × 85; 1734–52; 11 ×. Warburton, J. *London and Middlesex illustrated.* 1749. On a1. O (Gough Middlx. 13(10)). Condition: by 1752, badly worn. Variant: in *Reflections on gaming and observations relating thereto* (1733).

19 28 × 121; 1735–53; twice. *The philosophical transactions abridged.* Vol. VII, Pt. IV. 1735. On A1. O (Soc. 1996. d. 331/7 (i)). Signed 'FH'. Previous use: R. Walker, in *The countess's speech to her son Roderigo*, 2nd ed. (1731), and in *The city triumphant . . . A new ballad* (1733).

20 28 × 85; 1732–59; 24 ×. Lommius, J. *Treatise of continual fevers.* 1732. On L8. O (Vet. A4 e. 1764). Signed 'FH'. Condition: by 1740, trimmed both sides to width 82 mm. Previous use: W. Rayner, in *The whole of the proceedings . . . between the Hon. Mrs. Catherine Weld . . . and Edward Weld*, 1st, 2nd and 3rd eds. (1732), and in [Miller, J.] *Vanelia*, 6th ed. (1732). Variants: Richardson, in Defoe, D., *Tour through the whole island of Great Britain*, 2nd ed. (1738), I (not in Sale); Woodfall 66.

21 28 × 84; 1732–50; 8 ×. Overley, I. *The young gauger's instructor.* 1749. On B1. O (Vet. A4 e. 1738).

22 28 × 72; 1728–54; 27 ×. Ralph, J. *The muses' address to the king.* 1728. On a2. O (G. Pamph. 1286(2)). Condition: by 1728, notches in dark side-edges, lower left and upper right; by 1733, cut across man's shoulders. Previous use: SP, in Crowe (1720) to Thomas à Kempis (1727). Other use: Huggonson, in *Al Mesra* (1734) (or variant?). Variant: J. Watts, in Shadwell, T., *Dramatick works* (1720), I, on A8.

23 27 × 90; 1729–50; 12 ×. Ralph, J. *Clarinda.* 1729. On B1. O (Vet. A4 e. 763). Later use: by Townsend, in *A journal of the campaign on the coast of France* (1758). Variants: in Ellis, W., *Modern husbandman* (1750), II, on ^{2}B1; in Monoux, L., *A sermon preach'd at the triennial visitation . . . of Richard, Bishop of Lincoln* (1733), on B1 (larger, + 2 faces, 2 birds).

24★ 27 × 86; 1729; once. Source: as for 23. On C4^v. Signed 'FH'. Other use: (by W. or E. Rayner?), in [King, W.] *Ode to Myra* (1730) (cf. nos. 30★, 200★), and in Benson, G., *The end and design of prayer* (1731). Variant: Woodfall 45.

25 26.5 × 86.5; 1727–35; 9 ×. Potter, J. *A sermon preach'd at the coronation of King George II.* 1727. On B1. O (B 7. 20(4) Linc.). Condition: by 1728 split, near-vertical, just right of centre. Previous use: SP, in Henley (1720–26), no. 10 (1726). Variant: Richardson 19 (angel's flower larger).

26 26.5 × 83; 1748–51; 5 ×. Source: as for 18. On B1. Previous use: SP, from Juvenal & Persius (1728) to Greenup (1731), with frame complete on both sides. Variant: in Ovid, *Tristia* (1729), on B1.

27 25.5 × 75; 1728–47; 13 ×. Source: as for 22. On π3. Condition: by 1739, split in base of frame 12 mm from left corner. Previous use: SP, in E., R., *Exchange no robbery* (1718) to Thomas à Kempis (1727). Variant: in *The hyp, a burlesque poem* (1731).

28 25 × 134; 1735–59; 6 ×. Source: as for 11. On [A]4. Signed 'FH'. Condition: by 1735, outer frame damaged, above. Previous use: R. Walker, in *The countess's speech* (1731) (as for 19); S. Aris?, in Switzer, S., *An universal system of water and water-works* (1734). Variants: in Edwards, J., *Theologia reformata* (1726) on 3Z1; in *Ways and means for suppressing beggary* (1726).

29 25 × 83; 1734–40; 4 × . Source: as for 17. On B1. Signed 'FH'. Condition: by 1734, both sides of frame trimmed away. Previous use: SP, in Vossius (1724) to Chandler (1728). Variants: in Bradley, R., *New improvements of planting*, 4th ed. (1724), on 2C1; in Harte, W., *Poems on several occasions* (1727), on G5.

30★ 25 × 83; 1755; once. *The opposition*. 1755. O (G. Pamph. 1175(9)). On A3. Previous use: in [King, W.] (1730), on A5 (cf. nos. 24★, 200★).

31 24 × 72.5; 1733–55; 21 × . Thomson, G. *Anatomy of human bones*. 1734. On a1. O (Vet. A4 e. 2718).

32 24 × 69; 1731–54; 12 × . Ralph, B. *A new critical review of the publick buildings*. 2nd ed. 1736. On A4. O (Vet. A4 f. 303). Condition: by 1736, notch in lower horizontal of frame, 17 mm from left corner; upper left corner damaged.

33 23.5 × 72; 1732–54; 18 × . [Lockman, J.] *A new history of England*. 2nd ed. 1735. On A2. O (Vet. A4 f. 1749). Signed 'FH'. Condition: by 1735, notch in lower horizontal of frame, 28 mm from left corner. Previous use: SP, in Pitt (1725). Variants: Philipps, J. T. *A compendious way of teaching languages*, 3rd ed. (1728), on E2; J. Downing, in Johnston, S., *The advantage of employing the poor . . . a sermon*, 2nd ed. (1726); Woodfall 37.

34★ 23 × 86; 1729; once. Source: as for 23. On F1. Variants: in *New present state of England* (1750), II, on B1 (smaller).

35 23 × 80; 1728–54; 34 × . Source: as for 20. On A2. Previous use: SP, in Traile (1718) to Chandler (1725).

36 23 × 78.5; 1739–58; 7 × . Beeke, C. *The eucharistical sacrifice*. 1739. On B1. O (G. Pamph. 324(7)). Signed 'FH'. Previous use: by W. Rayner, in *Memoirs of the life of Robert Wilks*, 2nd ed. (1732); by him?, in [Fielding, Henry] *The genuine Grub-street opera* (1731).

37★ 22 × 71; 1754; once. Entick, J. *The pocket companion and history of free-masons*. 1754. On N9ᵛ. L (1486.aa.26). Signed 'FH'. Condition: worn. Previous use: Walker, in Pullen, J., *Memoirs of the maritime affairs of Great-Britain* (1732), on a1, F4; also (by W. or E. Rayner?) in 'Scriblerus Secundus' [Fielding, Henry] *The Welsh opera* (1731). Initials 'FH' clearly visible in 1731.

38 22 × 73; 1732–54; 3 × . Philipps, J. T. *A compendious way of teaching . . . languages*. 4th ed. 1750. On L3. O (Vet. A4 e. 2660). On L3. Condition: worn. Previous use: Rayner, in *The whole of the proceedings* (1732) (as for 20).

39★ 22 × 69; 1754; once. Source: as for 37★. On A3. Variant: J. Watts?, in Gay, J., *Poems on several occasions* (1745), II, on B2 (better quality).

40★ 21 × 108; 1734; once. Source: as for 19. Vol. VI, Pt. 1. 1734. On B1. O (Soc. 1996. d. 331/6 (i)).

41 21 × 79; 1729–56; 21 × . Source: as for 20. On B1. Condition: by 1750, lower left corner missing.

42 20 × 79; 1734–48; twice. Halfpenny, W. *Arithmetick and measurement, improv'd.* 1748. On B1. LUC (Graves 120. b. 3). Previous use: 'J.P.', in *Bob-lynn against Franck-lynn* (1732). Present in Pyle, T., *Paraphrase* (1750), I (use by CA?).

43 20 × 75; 1734–50; 10 ×. Source: as for 17. On R3. Signed 'FH'. Condition: by 1734, damage to right-hand bird's forward leg. Previous use: R. Walker, in *The progress of a harlot*, 2nd ed. (1732).

44 20 × 59; 1734–46; 5 ×. Haywood, E. *Secret histories, novels, and poems.* 4th ed. 1742. On IV, C8ᵛ. L (12614.c.13). Condition: by 1730, frame removed, trimmed and re-shaped. Previous use: SP, in Traile (1718), on X2ᵛ (within rectangular frame, 23 × 76), to Vida (1732).

45 19 × 86; 1742–50; 5 ×. Ellis, W. *A compleat system of experienced improvements.* 1749. On c4. L (35.a.23).

46★ 19 × 72; 1754; once. Source: as for 37★. On O2ᵛ. Variants: Watts?, in Gay (1745) (as for 39★), II, on C9 (better quality); Richardson 58.

47 19 × 68; 1733–55; 12 ×. Source: as for 31. On S5.

48 18.5 × 85; 1743–55; 4 ×. Morris, J. *Sermons on the following subjects.* 1743. On B1. C (6.29.40). Previous use: SP, in Ovid (1719) to *Comedian* (1732), VII. Variants: SP, in Gordon (1722), Boethius (1730), framed; in *The case of the insolvent debtors* (1728).

49 18.5 × 77; 1734–47; 7 ×. Pyle, T. *A paraphrase . . . on the acts of the apostles.* 2 vols. 3rd ed. 1737. On I, A5. O (Godw. 153 subt.).

50 18 × 73; 1742–54; 3 ×. Source: as for 37★. On P1. Variants: Watts?, in [Trapp, J.] *Abra-mule* (1735); W. Botham, in Clarke, S., *Demonstration of the being and attributes of God* (1732).

51 13 × 100; 1745–59; 16 ×. *LM.* February 1745. On H1. O (Hope Adds. 400). Monthly first page headpiece. Post-CA use: *LM*, May 1759–Dec. 1761, Jan. 1764. Variant: Cave in *Gentleman's magazine*, April 1738, on 2C5.

52 12 × 101; 1744; once (12 ×). *LM.* February 1744. On H1. O (Hope Adds. 399). Monthly first page headpiece, Feb.–Dec. 1744, + Appendix. Condition: by March, split near-vertically left of centre. Variants: Richardson 7, 8. Cp. Bowyer 95.

53 12 × 88; 1729–47; 24 ×. Source: as for 16. On D5. Condition: by 1743, diagonal split right of centre, and trimmed both sides.

54 12 × 83; 1734–59; 15 ×. Source: as for 21. On 2L3ᵛ. [CA use: 1734, once; 1749–59, 14 ×.] Previous use: by J. Redmayne, in B[ourne], V., *Carmina comitalia Cantabrigiensia* (1721). Variants: in Nepos, C., *Vitae excellentium imperatorum*, ed. and transl. J. Clarke (1723), on 2H1; W. Wilkins, in Hoadly, B., *An answer to . . . Dr. Hare's sermon* (1720), on O6ᵛ (−birds, +2 horns of flowers).

55 11 × 103; 1743–50; 5 ×. Source: as for 9. On π2. Condition: by 1747, trimmed at left; by 1748, split.

56 11 × 85; 1742–46; 3 ×. [Pelah, J.] *The mathematician*, no. II. 1746. On G2. O (Rigaud e. 292). Condition: by 1742, split vertically 2 mm left of centre.

57 11 × 77; 1737–56; 5 ×. Source: as for 49. On I, R2. Condition: by 1737, trimmed both sides. Previous use: Walker, in 'Scriblerus Quartus' [Cooke, T.] *The bays miscellany* (1730), on B3: untrimmed, 11 × 100; by W. or E. Rayner?, in *The coquet's surrender* (1732), for E. Rayner. Variants: in Newton, I., *Tables for leases of cathedral-churches*, 5th ed. (1735), on G3.

58 11 × 71; 1734–55; 26 ×. Source: as for 49. On I, L2. Variants: in Bradley, R., *A general treatise of husbandry and gardening* [2nd ed.] (1726), II, on 2B6; Bowyer 71.

59 10.5 × 81; 1735–54; twice. Source: as for 17. On 2D3. Condition: by 1754, vertical split 12 mm right of centre. Previous use: SP, in *Comedian* (1732), II.

60★ 10 × 90; 1748; once. Nepos, C. *Vitae excellentium imperatorum.* 7th ed. 1748. On 2I3ᵛ. CtY (Gnn40. g722g).

61 10 × 85; 1732–54; 7 ×. Source: as for 20. On A7. Condition: during 1732, split vertically 10 mm left of centre.

62★ 10 × 79; 1750; once. Gay, J. *The distress'd wife.* 2nd ed. 1750. On [A]1. L (643.g.10(1)). Previous use: SP, in Potter (1722).

63 10 × 72; 1732–55; 22 ×. Source: as for 20. On L2ᵛ. Condition: by 1749, trimmed to 10 × 66.

64 9 × 104; 1750–58; 9 ×. *LM.* 1753. On 4E1 (Appendix). O (Hope Adds. 408).

65 9 × 86; 1732–42; 7 ×. Source: as for 49. On I, F5.

66 9 × 85; 1734–51; 13 ×. Source: as for 49. On I, F7ᵛ.

67 8.5 × 83; 1737–54; 13 ×. Pascal, B. *Thoughts on religion.* 4th ed. 1749 (i.e., 4th ed., 1741, re-issued). On C3. O (Vet. A4 e. 917). Condition: trimmed on left side. Previous use: Walker, in 'Scriblerus Quartus' (1730) (as for 57), on D1ᵛ; Rayner, in *Memoirs . . . of Robert Wilks* (1732) (as for 36), on G4.

68 8 × 72; 1734–56; 9 ×. Source: as for 49. On I, C3.

69 7 × 70; 1735–46; 9 ×. Source: as for 33. On A4.

70 6.5 × 76; 1729–47; 17 ×. Source: as for 20. On A8. Previous use: SP, in Beveridge (1721); *All the wonders* (1722). Variants: Bowyer 79, 80; Wright 57.

71 6.5 × 75; 1734–54; 12 ×. Source: as for 49. On I, G2ᵛ. Condition: by 1749, left flower missing, 6.5 × 71.5.

72 6 × 77; 1734–37; twice. Source: as for 49. On I, B3. Condition: by 1734, small leaf trimmed off each lower corner (earlier: 6 × 78). Previous use: SP, in Beveridge (1721) to Chandler (1728). Used by Huggonson, in *Memoirs of the society of Grub-street* (1737), I, B6. Variants: Bowyer 77, 78, 87; Wright 46.

73 6 × 77; 1728–38; 12 ×. Hayes, R. *Interest at one view.* 1732. On A2. O (Vet. A4 g. 24). Previous use: SP, in Beveridge (1721) to Huet (1725).

74 6 × 76; 1728–49; 20 ×. Source: as for 49. On I, D2. Previous use: SP, in Beveridge (1721) to Ovid (1729). Variants: Bowyer 76, 86.

75 5 × 83; 1737–50; 9 ×. Source: as for 49. On I, C6. Previous use: SP, in Haywood (1730) to *Comedian* (1732), I.

76 5.5 × 66; 1746–54; 4 ×. Shakespeare, W. *Works*. 1747. Vol. VIII. On N1. L (11764.a.13). Condition: trimmed from original length, *ca.*80 mm, with removal of flower at either end; split left of central horseshoe; in 1754 (in item **315**) broken centre of this orn. is combined with shortened 78, to make *ad hoc* headpiece. Previous use: Walker?, in 'Scriblerus Quartus' (1730) (as for 57), and in *Some useful and occasional remarks on a late seditious libel* (1731).

77 5 × 87; 1742–55; 4 ×. Nepos, C. *Vitae excellentium imperatorum*. 8th ed. 1754. On X3ᵛ. O (Vet. A5 e. 4224). Previous use: SP, in Nepos (1720) to Henley (1720–26), no. 10 (1726).

78 5 × 81; 1737–58; 13 ×. Source: as for 49. On I, A6. Condition: by 1754 trimmed both sides to 5 × 69 (see 76). Previous use: SP, in *Comedian* (1732), V. Variant: Bowyer 93 (deeper).

79 5 × 80.5; 1728–32; 11 ×. Gonson, J. *Charge to the grand jury of Westminster* [3 July 1729]. 1729. On A2. O (Pamph. 385(3)). Previous use: SP, in Guillim (1726). Variant: Bowyer 95 (larger, better quality).

80★ 5 × 78; 1750; once. Source: as for 62★. On [A]1. Used in Pyle, T., *Paraphrase* (1750), I (by CA?).

81 5 × 60; 1746–47; twice. Source: as for 76. On N2. Condition: vertical split both sides, trimmed at left. Previous use: Walker?, in 'Scriblerus Quartus' (1730) (as for 57), on B2 (already split on left side). Variants: Bowyer 86; Wright 34.

Tailpieces

82 58 × 63; 1728–35; 11 ×. Philipps, J. T. *Epistolae laconicae*. 1729. On A4. O (29696 f. 7). Condition: by 1728, thin line through sun's rays, right. Previous use: SP, in Traile (1718), on S7ᵛ, to Wollaston (1731), on 2E4 (borrowed back by SP, or borrowed forward by CA?). Variants: reproduction, no provenance, in Carol Benton Grafton, *Pictorial archives of printers' ornaments from the Renaissance to the twentieth century* (New York, 1980), p. 33; in others, sun has face.

83 57 × 72; 1728–50; 23 ×. Ralph, J. *Night*. 1728. On D3. O (Vet. A4 e. 162(10)). Previous use: SP, in Sprat (1722) to Chandler (1725). Variants: Watts?, in Gay, J., *Poems on several occasions* (1720), II, on 2O4ᵛ; in Humphreys, S., *Cannons. A poem* (1728), on G1.

84 52 × 76; 1733–43; 4 ×. Source: as for 3. On A4ᵛ. Previous use: SP, in La Mottraye, III (1732).

85 52 × 64; 1732–52; 17 ×. Source: as for 31. On c4. Previous use: SP, in Traile (1718) to *Comedian* (1732), VI.

86 51 × 62.5; 1728–56; 21 ×. Source: as for 22. On a4. Previous use: SP, in Lisle (1723) to Selden (1725–26), II (1), on 5Y2ᵛ.

87 46 × 55; 1732–56; 17 ×. *LM*. 1732. On 4C4 (Appendix). O (Hope Adds. 387). Signed 'FH'. Previous use: SP, in Mitchell (1720) to Chandler (1728). Variants: in *Milton's Paradise lost, or,* *the fall of man* [paraphrased by] Raymond [or rather N. F. Dupré] de Saint Maur (1755), on 2A1ᵛ; J. Barber, in Sheffield, J., *Works* (1723), II, on Q4; in Fiddes, R., *Life of Wolsey* (1726).

88 46 × 53; 1731–50; 20 × . Source: as for 3. On C4ᵛ·

89 45 × 61; 1733–57; 8 × . Source: as for 31. On M3. Previous use: SP, in Lamy (1723) to Wollaston (1731). Imitates design in Saurin, J., *Discours historiques, critiques, theologiques, et moraux* (Amsterdam, 1720).

90 45 × 60; 1735–48; 3 × . *LM.* 1735. On 5D3. O (Hope Adds. 390). Previous use: SP (his device), in Traile (1718) to *Comedian* (1732), VI.

91 45 × 52; 1734–55; 10 × . Source: as for 31. On U6. Previous use: SP, in Coles (1718) to *Comedian* (1732), VII. Variants: Barber, in Sheffield (1723) (as for 87), II, on Z2 (finer quality); in *An exact list of the knights* (1722), on T5ᵛ (reversed).

92 43 × 56; 1734–59; 14 × . Source: as for 17. On R1ᵛ. Previous use: Walker?, in *The city triumphant* (1733) (as for 19), on [B]2ᵛ. Variants: in Bradley (1724) (as for 29), on A8ᵛ; in same, on N4; in Hayes, R., *Rules for the port of London* (1722), on G1.

93★ 43 × 64; 1735; once. Tatersal, R. *The bricklayer's miscellany*, 2nd part. 1735. On D4. O (G. Pamph. 1287(16)). Previous use: J. Chrichley, in Cooke, T., *Letters of Atticus, as printed in the London journal, 1729* (1730), on I4; Huggonson, in Pope [1733] (as for 3). Variant: in *A letter to William Pulteney, Esq.* (1733), on C2ᵛ (better quality).

94 42 × 64; 1729–54; 36 × . Source: as for 7. On A1. Previous use: SP, in Beveridge (1721); also, central element used separately, in Ditton (1722).

95★ 40 × 66; 1742; once. Elliston, R. *Officia sacrata.* 1742. On a4. NN (★KC. 1742).

96 39 × 52; 1733–44; 19 × . Source: as for 17. On 2O3ᵛ. Previous use: SP, in *Comedian* (1732), II.

97 37 × 58; 1752–56; twice. Source: as for 6. On a1ᵛ. Previous use: in [Browne, I. H.] *The fire-side: a pastoral soliloquy* [1746]. Variants: Bowyer 144 (finer quality); in *The unembarassed countenance, a new ballad* (1746); in Barham, H., *An essay on the silkworm* (1719).

98 37 × 39; 1735–59; 4 × . Ellis, W. *The practical farmer.* 5th ed. 1759. On O3. L (235.g.31). Previous use: W. Rayner?, in *An excise elegy* (1733), and in *The miter* [ca.1730] (as for 12).

99 36 × 59; 1733–51; 5 × . Source: as for 18. On Y4. Previous use: SP, in Traile (1718) to *Comedian* (1732), III. Variants: Bowyer 151 (mirror image); Richardson 66, 67; in Lancaster, N., *Public virtue . . . A sermon* (1746).

100 34 × 65.5; 1728–42; 19 × . Source: as for 83. On E4. Previous use: SP, in *Biblia sacra* (1726), IV.

101 34 × 31; 1734–56; 9 × . Source: as for 31. On R2. Used by Townsend, in *Journal* (1758) (as for 23).

102 33.5 × 50; 1735–55; 15 × . Source: as for 49. On I, A5ᵛ. Signed 'FH' (damaged). Previous use: SP, in Beveridge (1721) to Croft (1730).

103 31 × 44; 1731–56; 35 × . Source: as for 20. On L7^v. Used by Townsend, in *Journal* (1758) (as for 23). Post-CA use: *LM General Index* (1760), on Bb4. Variant: Wright 3.

104★ 29 × 46; 1729; once. Source: as for 23. On C4. Signed 'FH' (damaged). Previous use: in Calamy, E., *The word of God* (1725), on D3^v; and in *The bachelor's estimate of the expence of a married life*, 3rd ed. (1729). Variant: Woodfall 228, signed 'F. Hoffman'.

105 29 × 33; 1733–43; 8 × . Source: as for 33. On A3^v. Previous use: in Vida, *Poemata* (1730), Part II. Variants: Bowyer 176; R. Harbin, in Ovid, *Epistolarum heroidum* (1722), on π2.

106 28.5 × 41; 1733–59; 31 × . Source: as for 36. On M7. Used by Townsend, in *Journal* (1758) (as for 23).

107 28 × 42; 1729–32; 8 × . Source: as for 20. On L2. Variants: Wright 26 (smaller); in Monoux (1733) (as for 23), on C8^v (+ 2 flying birds, signed 'FH').

108 25 × 55; 1728–55; 10 × . Bedford, A. *Animadversions*. 1728. On A4^v. O (8º F 238 Linc.). Variants: Watts, 1718–35; in [Brady & Tate] *A new version of the Psalms* (1764) (−foliage, + 'FINIS' on banner).

109 25 × 37.5; 1734–54; 16 × . Source: as for 49. On I, T7. Previous use: SP, in Ramsay (1731), II, to Vida (1732); Huggonson, in Pope [1733] (as for 3). Variant: Walker?, in *Some objections humbly offered to the . . . House of Commons* (1729).

110 25 × 37; 1733–54; 24 × . Source: as for 3. On E1^v. Variant: in periodical *The old maid*, issues 1, 5, 6, 9, 28, 29 (1755–56).

111 25 × 32; 1729–55; 20 × . Ralph, J. *Miscellaneous poems, by several hands*. 1729. On C3^v. O (Radcliffe f. 218). Previous use: SP, in Allestree (1720) to Chandler (1728). Variant: Bowyer 177.

112 24 × 44; 1735–43; 4 × . *LM*. 1739. On 4I2^v. O (Hope Adds. 394). Previous use: SP, in Ovid (1719) to Ovid (1730).

113★ 24 × 31; 1734; once. Source: as for 2★. On 6E1^v. Previous use: in Jebb, S., ed., *Joanni Caii de canibus Britannicis* (1729). Status dubious. Used in Stackhouse (item **404**) in conjunction with no. 163, but in a part of the book possibly printed by James Bettenham.

114 23 × 23; 1739–49; 6 × . Source: as for 48. On O7^v.

115 22 × 34; 1734–35; twice. Bailey, N. *English and Latin exercises*. 9th ed. 1734. On A3. MH (GutmanEduc.T.20917.34).

116 20 × 27; 1734–56; 6 × . Source: as for 31. On S7. Previous use: SP, in Boethius (1730) to *Comedian* (1732), II. Variant: Walker?, in [Haywood, E.] *The fair hebrew* (1729), on [A]2^v.

117 19.5 × 36; 1735–59; 26 × . Source: as for 31. On Y2^v. Post-CA use: *LM General Index* (1760), on A1.

118 19 × 26; 1731–55; 11 × . Source: as for 17. On R3. Signed 'FH'. Variants: Huggonson, in Browne, I. H., *A pipe of tobacco* (1736); Richardson?, in *Debates in the House of Commons* (1742), I.

119 15 × 29; 1733–49; 9 × . Source: as for 3. On C4. Variant: in Cooke, T., *The triumphs of love and honour* (1731) (larger, poorer quality).

120 14 × 41; 1731–54; 19 ×. Source: as for 20. On A8ᵛ.

121★ 10 × 29; 1742; once. Source: as for 95★. On 2B1ᵛ.

122 10 × 22; 1732–42; 6 ×. Source: as for 3. On D1.

123 9 × 47; 1735–56; 6 ×. Source: as for 49. On I, X3. Condition: by 1735, presumably substantially trimmed.

Initials

124 37 × 37; 1733–59; 4 ×. Source: as for 3. On D1.

125 37 × 37; 1734–53; 3 ×. Source: as for 2★. On a1.

126 37 × 37; 1733–42; twice. Source: as for 3. On E3ᵛ.

127 33 × 32; 1728–59; 21 ×. Source: as for 22. On a2. Condition: by 1724 (SP use), notched in lower frame 13 mm from left. Previous use: SP, in Henley (1720–26), no. 7 (1721), to Wollaston (1725). Variants: SP, in Wollaston (1726), on A2 (finer quality, Hercules facing half right), same used by Huggonson, in Swift, J., *On poetry* (1733); in Welsted, L., *A prologue to the town* (1721), on B1 (sparser).

128 34 × 32; 1727–50; 6 ×. Source: as for 25. On B1. Previous use: SP, in Lisle (1723) to Wollaston (1726). Variant: SP, in *Grub-street journal* (1730) to La Mottraye (1732), III (in better condition); used by Huggonson, in *The free Briton*, no. 168, 15 February 1733.

129 34 × 32; 1733–59; 4 ×. Source: as for 11. On D4. Previous use: SP, in Lamy (1723) to Palmer (1732).

130 31 × 31; 1733–59; 5 ×. Source: as for 3. On D3.

131 31 × 32; 1733–35; twice. Source: as for 3. On D4.

132★ 28.5 × 25; 1750; once. Source: as for 38. On C3. Previous use: SP, in Leybourn (1722) to Chandler (1728).

133★ 28 × 25; 1739; once. Source: as for 36. On M4ᵛ. Signed 'FH'.

134 29 × 25; 1742–53; twice. Source: as for 64. On a1.

135 29 × 26.5; 1747–50; twice. Source: as for 16. On B1. Previous use: SP [Huggonson], in *Comedian* (1732), VIII; Huggonson, in *The free Briton*, no. 170, 1 March 1733.

136 26 × 23; 1729–58; 25 ×. Source: as for 23. On C4ᵛ. Previous use: SP, in Leybourn (1722). Condition: in 1722, 29 × 24.5; by 1729, outer frame damaged, lower right; thereafter, trimmed away.

137 27 × 23.5; 1733–59; 4 ×. Source: as for 3. On D1ᵛ.

138 29 × 25.5; 1733–59; 12 ×. Source: as for 17. On 2D3. Previous use: SP, in Henley (1720–26), no. 8 (1722), to Salignac (1729); Huggonson, in *The free Briton*, no. 169, 22 February 1733.

139 29 × 27; 1733–59; 4 × . Source: as for 3. On E1. Previous use: SP, in Beveridge (1721) to Henley (1720–26), no. 8 (1722).

140 28 × 25; 1733–47; 3 × . Source: as for 3. On E1ᵛ. Previous use: SP, in Ramsay (1721) to Edwards (1726); Huggonson, in *The free Briton*, no. 159, 14 December 1732.

141 28 × 25; 1729–59; 15 × . Source: as for 7. On B1. Previous use: SP, in *The yea and nay stock-jobbers* (1720) to Guillim (1726).

142 25 × 25; 1733–59; 12 × . Source: as for 9. On π2. Previous use: SP, in Braine, 2nd ed. (1724) to *Comedian* (1732), II; Huggonson, in *The free Briton*, no. 176, 5 April 1733.

143 24.5 × 26; 1733–59; 17 × . Source: as for 3. On A3.

144 23.5 × 24; 1732–50; 10 × . Source: as for 16. On A2.

145 22 × 22; 1728–56; 42 × . Source: as for 108. On A2. Signed 'FH'. Previous use: SP, in Ovid (1724). Post-CA use: *LM*, 1760.

146 20.5 × 20; 1747–50; twice. Source: as for 16. On K3ᵛ.

147★ 20 × 20; 1729; once. Ralph, J. *Miscellaneous poems* (*Night*, 2nd ed.). 1729. On C3. L (992. k.15(1)).

148 19 × 20; 1732–49; 21 × . Source: as for 16. On A3ᵛ. Variant: Woodfall 376, T4.

149 17 × 16.5; 1732–56; 14 × . Source: as for 67. On C3.

150★ 17 × 16; 1746; once. Kimber, I. *The history of England*. 1755. (Re-issue of 1746 ed.). On F6ᵛ. O (Vet. A5 e. 3126).

151 17 × 17; 1732–58; 7 × . Source: as for 73. On A2.

152 17 × 16.5; 1732–52; 16 × . Source: as for 18. On B1.

153 16 × 16; 1732–53; 17 × . Source: as for 11. On I4.

Factotums

154 36 × 35; 1733–59; 6 × . Source: as for 3. On D2. Previous use: SP, in [Nevil] (1717) to *Grub-street journal*, 19 May 1730. Variant: in *Bickerton's journal*, issue 11 of June 1715 (current title: *The Church-man's last shift*). Cp. Bowyer 201.

155 34 × 31; 1735–59; 5 × . Source: as for 11. On E3ᵛ.

156 32 × 29; 1729–41; 11 × . Source: as for 23. On F1.

157 31 × 31; 1731–59; 15 × . Source: as for 3. On A2. Variants: Ackers 158; Wright xi.

158 29.5 × 23; 1731–59; 19 × . Source: as for 18. On a1. Variants: in *London courant*, 1733–45; Ackers 157; SP, in Thomas à Kempis (1727).

159 29 × 29; 1728–59; 16 × . Source: as for 3. On C3. Signed 'FH'. Previous use: SP, in Kinch (1722).

160 29 × 27; 1732–59; 18 ×. Source: as for 20. On B1. Signed 'FH' (in flower centres).

161 27.5 × 28; 1735–59; 7 ×. Source: as for 14. On π2. Signed 'FH'. Previous use: Walker, in Pullen (1732) (as for 37★), and in *A short and pithy sermon . . . against slavery and wooden shoes* (1733).

162 27 × 25; 1743–59; 17 ×. Source: as for 9. On A1. Post-CA use: *LM*, 1760–62, 1764.

163 27 × 25; 1728–34; 7 ×. Source: as for 22. On B1. Previous use: in Hendley, W., *Defence of the charity-schools* (1725).

164 26 × 24; 1729–59; 18 ×. Source: as for 111. On A2.

165 25 × 24; 1729–43; 16 ×. Source: as for 20. On A2. Used regularly for *Weekly register*, 1730–31.

166 24.5 × 24; 1729–59; 20 ×. Source: as for 82. On B1. Used regularly for *Weekly register*, 1731–35. Condition: inner square progressively disappears. Used in Pyle, T., *Paraphrase* (1750), I (by CA?).

167 20 × 23.5; 1730; once. *Weekly register*, no. xii, 3 July 1730. O (NN 71c(286)). Used for advertisement for cockfighting at the Red-Lyon Cockpit, Clerkenwell. Other use: for same purpose, in *The daily post-boy*, no. 6646, 27 June 1730, printed by W. Marsh, and in some other issues to 1733.

168 20 × 20; 1731–59; 37 ×. Source: as for 3. On C4ᵛ. Used monthly for *LM*, 1732–49. Post-CA use: *LM*, 1761–62. Variants: in *Reasons for further explanations . . . of . . . an act for the relief of debtors* (1731); in *Fog's weekly journal*, e.g., issue of 20 June 1730.

169 20 × 20; 1729–36; 13 ×. Source: as for 20. On L8. Variants: Bowyer 214; in Ellis, W., *The timber-tree improved* (1742), on B1; Huggonson?, in *Al Mesra* (1734); in *Fog's weekly journal* (1730).

170★ 20 × 19; 1755; once. Source: as for 30★. On A3.

171★ 20 × 19; 1730; once. [Newton, W.] *The life of Dr. Kennett* (1730). On P3ᵛ. C (Peterborough V.2.43).

172 20 × 18; 1742–59; 8 ×. Source: as for 11. On E1. Previous use: Say, in Carey (1729) (as for 33), on P2.

173 20 × 18; 1752–59; 8 ×. Source: as for 6. On G2. Post-CA use: *LM*, 1759–61. Variants: Bowyer 230; Cave, in *Gentleman's magazine*, e.g., 1738, on 2M2; Watts?, in Cooke, T., *The mournful nuptials* (1739), on B1; in H., W., *Hermes romanus*, 7th ed. (1750).

174 19 × 19; 1734–59; 27 ×. Source: as for 31. On A2. Previous use: SP, in Milner (1729); Huggonson, in *The free Briton*, no. 131, 25 May 1732, to no. 158, 7 December 1732. Condition: by 1740, notch in right vertical of inner frame. Variant: Bowyer 230.

175 19 × 19; 1732–50; 16 ×. Source: as for 150★. On L4ᵛ. Previous use: SP, in *The free Briton*, no. 40, 3 September 1730, to Palmer (1732), on 2R1.

176 19 × 18; 1735–59; 10 ×. Source: as for 11. On F4. Previous use: SP, in Coles (1718) to

Boulainvilliers (1731). Variant: T. Browne, in Masters, M., *Poems on several occasions* (1733) (head below slot).

177 18.5 × 16.5; 1732–48; 15 × . Source: as for 31. On S5. Previous use: SP, in Vossius (1724) to *Grub-street journal*, 21 January 1731. Other use: Huggonson, in *The free Briton*, no. 161, 28 December 1732. Condition: by 1747, battered. Used by Huggonson (borrowed?), in *Memoirs of the society of Grub-street* (1737), I, on B1. Variants: Bowyer 205; Richardson?, in *Some considerations humbly offered to the hon. House of Commons* (1732); in *The eagle* (1723); in Ovid, *Metamorphoseon* (1730), on R7^v.

178 18 × 18; 1742–59; 6 × . Source: as for 11. On D2^v. Signed 'FH'. Previous use: Say, in Carey (1729) (as for 33), on 2D3^v.

179★ 18 × 17.5; 1746; once. Source: as for 150★. On T8^v. Variant: Watts?, in Southern, T., *Works* (1721), II, on P3.

180 18 × 17; 1732–49; 16 × . Source: as for 33. On A4. Previous use: SP, in *The free Briton*, no. 88, 5 August 1731 to Vida (1732). Variants: Walker, in [Haywood, E.] *The fair hebrew*, 1st and 2nd eds. (1729); Watts, in Shadwell (1720) (as for 22), II, on D6; W. Roberts, in *Missionalia* (1728).

181 18 × 17; 1742; twice. Nepos, C. *Vitae excellentium imperatorum.* 6th ed. 1742. On E1^v. CtY (1974. 2290).

182★ 18 × 15; 1748; once. Source: as for 60★. On E1^v.

183 17.5 × 17.5; 1752–59; 8 × . Source: as for 6. On F1. Post-CA use: *LM*, 1759–60.

184 17.5 × 17.5; 1732–59; 23 × . Source: as for 11. On D4^v. Previous use: SP, in [Mottley, J.] *The craftsman . . . a farce* (1729); in *Grub-street journal*, 1730–32, including use by Huggonson after SP's death. Other use: by Huggonson, in *The free Briton*, to no. 174, 22 March 1733. Used by Townsend, in *Journal* (1758) (as for 23). Post-CA use: *LM*, 1761–62.

185★ 17.5 × 17; 1751; once. Jeffries, D. *Treatise on diamonds and pearls.* 2nd ed. (1751). On B1. O (Douce J 182).

186 17 × 17; 1731–56; 38 × . Source: as for 17. On R3. Variants: Ackers 193, 194.

187★ 17 × 16; 1746; once. Source: as for 150★. On N4. Variant: Bowyer 234.

188★ 17 × 16; 1746; once. Source: as for 150★. On M5^v.

189★ 17 × 16; 1742; once. Source: as for 181. On B2.

190★ 17 × 16; 1746; once. Source: as for 150★. On R1.

191★ 17 × 16; 1746; once. Source: as for 150★. On O8.

192★ 17 × 16; 1748; once. Source: as for 60★. On F4^v.

193 16.5 × 17; 1742; twice. Dyche, T. *Guide to the English tongue.* 28th ed. 1742. On A2. BN. Variants: Ackers 186, 194.

194 16.5 × 17; 1732–45; 14 × . Source: as for 87. On E2^v. Variants: Ackers 186, 193.

195★ 16.5 × 16.5; 1742; once. Source: as for 181. On C2.

196★ 16.5 × 16; 1742; once. Source: as for 181. On B2. Variant: Bowyer 238.

197 16.5 × 16; 1734–54; 19 ×. Source: as for 150★. On H8. Previous use: SP, in Wollaston (1731), on 2F1. Other use: by Huggonson, in *The free Briton*, to no. 173, 15 March 1733. Variant: W. Roberts, in *Missionalia* (1728), on I1.

198 16 × 17; 1732–34; 3 ×. Source: as for 87. On 2T2ᵛ.

199 16 × 17; 1732–59; 34 ×. Source: as for 20. On L2ᵛ.

200★ 16 × 16; 1742; once. Source: as for 181. On C2. Previous use: in [King, W.] *Ode to Myra* (1730) (cf. nos. 24★, 30★).

201 16 × 16; 1744–59; 17 ×. Source: as for 38. On H7ᵛ. Variant: in Haywood, E. (1742) (as for 44), I, on B1 (Ackers printed Vols. III and IV of this edition).

202 15 × 15; 1742; twice. Source: as for 44. On IV, F2.

203 15 × 15; 1729–49; 18 ×. Source: as for 33. On A2. Previous use: SP, in Beveridge (1721) to *Grub-street journal*, 16 July 1730.

204★ 13.5 × 13; 1749; once. *LM*. 1749. On 3Q2. C (T900.d.1.18). Variant: Bowyer 195 (larger).

Devices

205★ 59 × 84; 1745; once. *A new general collection of voyages and travels*. 1745–47. On I, A1ᵛ. O (GG 29 Jur.). (In *Ledger*, Appendix I, under 'Collection'.) Royal arms, above licence.

206★ 48 × 64; 1754; once. Source: as for 37★. On [A]2. Dedicatee's heraldic device (i.e., of Sir John Proby, first Baron Carysfort).

207 47 × 42.5; 1728–48: twice. Source: as for 108. On A1. Though presumably cut as Ackers' device ('CA'), it is not known to have been used elsewhere.

208 35 × 50; 1750–51; twice. Phaedrus. *Phaedri fabulae*. 5th ed. 1750. On π1ᵛ. ICU (Regenstein. LT. PA6563. A238. 1750). Royal arms, above licence.

Engravings Used as Ornaments

209 66.5 × 107 (68 × 109); 1732–45; 14 ×. Source: as for 87. On π1. On annual title-page from 1732 on. Words 'J. Pine fecit.' disappeared after 1735. Measurements in brackets are those of frame of rules.

210★ 34.5 × 71; 1729; once. Source: as for 111. On A2. Dedicatee's heraldic device (i.e., of the Earl of Albemarle).

211 60 × 118; 1733; twice. Martyn, B. *Reasons for establishing the colony of Georgia*. 2nd ed. 1733. On F1. O (Pamph. 400(12)). 'I. Pine De. et Sculp.'

SECTION IV

Analyses

(1) Chronological Listing of Ornaments by First Appearance

D = device; E = engraving; F = factotum; H = headpiece; I = initial; T = tailpiece.
SA = Samuel Aris; JC = John Chrichley; JH = John Huggonson; SP = Samuel Palmer;
JP = John Purser; WR = William (and E.?) Rayner; Re = James Redmayne; JR = James
Roberts; ES = Edward Say; RW = Robert Walker.

25H	1727–35	SP		111T	1729–55	SP
128I	1727–50	SP		136I	1729–58	SP
10H	1728–52			141I	1729–59	SP
22H	1728–54	SP		147★I	1729	
27H	1728–47	SP		156F	1729–41	
35H	1728–54	SP		164F	1729–59	
73H	1728–38	SP		165F	1729–43	
74H	1728–49	SP		166F	1729–59	
79H	1728–32	SP		169F	1729–36	
82T	1728–35	SP		203F	1729–49	SP
83T	1728–50	SP		210★E	1729	
86T	1728–56	SP		167F	1730	
100T	1728–42	SP		171★F	1730	
108T	1728–55			32H	1731–54	
127I	1728–59	SP		88T	1731–50	
145I	1728–56	SP		103T	1731–56	
159F	1728–59	SP		118T	1731–55	
163F	1728–34			120T	1731–54	
207D	1728–48			157F	1731–59	
7H	1729–34	JR?		158F	1731–59	
23H	1729–50			168F	1731–59	
24★H	1729			186F	1731–56	
34★H	1729	SP		20H	1732–59	WR
41H	1729–56			21H	1732–50	
53H	1729–47			33H	1732–54	SP
70H	1729–47	SP		38H	1732–54	WR?
94T	1729–54	SP		61H	1732–54	
104★T	1729			63H	1732–55	
107T	1729–32			65H	1732–42	

53

85T	1732–52	SP		17H	1734–59	SP/JH
87T	1732–56	SP		18H	1734–52	
122T	1732–42			29H	1734–40	SP
144I	1732–50			40★H	1734	
148I	1732–49			42H	1734–48	JP
149I	1732–56			43H	1734–50	RW
151I	1732–58			44H	1734–46	SP
152I	1732–52			49H	1734–47	
153I	1732–53			54H	1734–59	Re
160F	1732–59			58H	1734–55	
175F	1732–50	SP		66H	1734–51	
177F	1732–48	SP/JH		68H	1734–56	
180F	1732–49	SP		71H	1734–54	
184F	1732–59	SP/JH		72H	1734–37	SP
194F	1732–45			91T	1734–55	SP
198F	1732–34			92T	1734–59	RW?
199F	1732–59			101T	1734–56	
209E	1732–45			109T	1734–54	SP/JH
3H	1733–38	SP/JH		113★T	1734	
16H	1733–55	SP		115T	1734–35	
31H	1733–55			116T	1734–56	SP
47H	1733–55			125I	1734–53	
84T	1733–43	SP		174F	1734–59	SP/JH
89T	1733–57	SP		197F	1734–54	SP/JH
96T	1733–44	SP		19H	1735–53	RW
99T	1733–51	SP		28H	1735–59	RW/ SA?
105T	1733–43			59H	1735–54	SP
106T	1733–59			69H	1735–46	
110T	1733–54			90T	1735–48	SP
119T	1733–49			93★T	1735	JC/JH
124I	1733–59			98T	1735–59	WR?
126I	1733–42			102T	1735–55	SP
129I	1733–59	SP		112T	1735–43	SP
130I	1733–59			117T	1735–59	
131I	1733–35			123T	1735–56	
137I	1733–59			155F	1735–59	
138I	1733–59	SP/JH		161F	1735–59	RW
139I	1733–59			176F	1735–59	SP
140I	1733–47	SP/JH		57H	1737–56	RW/ WR?
142I	1733–59	SP/JH		67H	1737–54	RW?/ WR
143I	1733–59			75H	1737–50	SP
154F	1733–59	SP		78H	1737–58	SP
211E	1733			36H	1739–58	WR
2★H	1734			114T	1739–49	
12H	1734–50	WR		133★I	1739	

15★H	1740	JR?
45H	1742–50	
50H	1742–54	
56H	1742–46	
77H	1742–55	SP
95★T	1742	
121★T	1742	
134I	1742–53	
172F	1742–59	ES
178F	1742–59	ES
181F	1742	
189★F	1742	
193F	1742	
195★F	1742	
196★F	1742	
200★F	1742	
202F	1742	
9H	1743–59	
48H	1743–55	SP
55H	1743–50	
162F	1743–59	
52H	1744	
201F	1744–59	
51H	1745–59	
205★D	1745	
1H	1746–47	
13★H	1746	
14H	1746–58	
76H	1746–54	RW?
81H	1746–47	RW?
150★I	1746	
179★F	1746	
187★F	1746	
188★F	1746	
190★F	1746	
191★F	1746	
135I	1747–50	SP/JH
146I	1747–50	
5H	1748–52	
26H	1748–51	SP
60★H	1748	
182★F	1748	
192★F	1748	
204★F	1749	
62★H	1750	SP
64H	1750–58	
80★H	1750	
132★I	1750	SP
208D	1750–51	
185★F	1751	
6H	1752–56	
97T	1752–56	
173F	1752–59	
183F	1752–59	
8★H	1753	
11H	1753–59	
37★H	1754	RW/ WR?
39★H	1754	
46★H	1754	
206★D	1754	
30★H	1755	
170★F	1755	
4H	1757–59	

(2) Totals for years

1727	1 × H, 1 × I (2)
1728	7 × H, 5 × T, 2 × I, 2 × F, 1 × D (17)
1729	7 × H, 4 × T, 3 × I, 6 × F, 1 × E (21)
1730	2 × F
1731	1 × H, 4 × T, 4 × F (9)
1732	7 × H, 3 × T, 6 × I, 8 × F, 1 × E (25)
1733	4 × H, 8 × T, 11 × I, 1 × F, 1 × E (25)
1734	16 × H, 7 × T, 1 × I, 2 × F (26)
1735	4 × H, 7 × T, 3 × F (14)
1737	4 × H
1739	1 × H, 1 × T, 1 × I
1740	1 × H
1742	4 × H, 2 × T, 1 × I, 9 × F (16)
1743	3 × H, 1 × F
1744	1 × H, 1 × F
1745	1 × H, 1 × D
1746	5 × H, 1 × I, 5 × F (11)
1747	2 × I

1748	$3 \times H$, $2 \times F$		1753	$2 \times H$
1749	$1 \times F$		1754	$3 \times H$, $1 \times D$
1750	$3 \times H$, $1 \times I$, $1 \times D$		1755	$1 \times H$, $1 \times F$
1751	$1 \times F$		1757	$1 \times H$
1752	$1 \times H$, $1 \times T$, $2 \times F$			

(3) Provenance, from other printers

Samuel Palmer: 3, 16, 17, 22, 25, 26, 27, 29, 33, 34★, 35, 44, 48, 59, 62★, 70, 72, 73, 74, 75, 77, 78, 79, 82, 83, 84, 85, 86, 87, 89, 90, 91, 94, 96, 99, 100, 102, 109, 111, 112, 116, 127, 128, 129, 132★, 135, 136, 138, 140, 141, 142, 145, 154, 159, 174, 175, 176, 177, 180, 184, 197, 203.

John Huggonson: (a) from Palmer: 3, 17, 109, 135, 138, 140, 142, 174, 177, 184, 197; (b) from John Chrichley: 93★.

Robert Walker: 19, 28, 37★, 43, 57, 67?, 76?, 81?, 92?, 161.

William (and E.?) Rayner: 12, 20, 36, 38?, 67, 98? [Some sharing, e.g., 67, and possibly also 37★ and 57, with RW?]

Edward Say: 172, 178.

James Roberts(?): 7, 15★?

James Redmayne: 54.

J.P. (John Purser?): 42.

Samuel Aris?: possibly used 28, between RW and Ackers.

Unidentified: 8★, 24★, 30★, 97, 104★, 105, 113★, 163, 200★.

(4) Classification by Graphic Elements

To the schema outlined by James Mitchell (see Section 1, and note 10), is added the division between framed and unframed ornaments, for each broad class (headpieces, tailpieces, initials, factotums).

Rectangular-shaped scenes with an outlined edge but not an integrated frame-structure are considered unframed. Bundles containing words or letters (usually the cutter's initials) are listed separately, but also included within the two main sequences. Within these sequences the bundles are classified in terms of their main central elements, and initially divided into:

(I) those with an element above an element above an element;
(II) those with an element above an element;
(III) those with nothing above or below the central element.

With initials and factotums the mid-level elements may be either side of the central letter or slot.

Only a few subjects are numerous enough to merit further subdivision in relation to elements to left and right. Containers (basket, bowl, horn, vase, etc.) may contain flowers (C:fl), fruit (C:fr) or both (C:fl + fr). I have used 'Scene' to denote anything constituting a 'picture', whether landscape or human figures are dominant within it. Plausible secondary classifications are put within square brackets.

Initials

Factotums

APPENDIX I

Ackers' Books: Addenda and Corrigenda

THIS section comprises addenda and corrigenda to McKenzie and Ross, *A ledger of Charles Ackers* (1968), Appendix I. It emends existing entries, and adds 58 items not included in the original series, though some were listed by author and short title in the 'Addenda' section (p. 317). They are inserted in alphabetical order, and given the number of the preceding item, plus 'A', etc. They have been identified as coming from Ackers' printing-house either by their imprints or by the evidence of ornaments. For some addenda and corrigenda I am indebted to Mr David Foxon's review in *The library*, 5th ser., 25 (1970), 65–73, where they are often spelt out in greater detail than here. For the imprints, the conventions have been adopted of omitting the place of publication (London) and of giving the date of issue before the names of booksellers. Digraphs in titles have been expanded to 'ae' and 'oe'.

2A Ainsworth, R. *Thesaurus linguae Latinae compendiarius: or, a compendious dictionary of the Latin tongue.* 2 vols. 3rd ed. 1751. Printed by C. and J. Ackers, for W. Mount and T. Page, W. Innys, R. Ware, J. and P. Knapton, T. Cox, T. Longman, C. Hitch, A. Millar, J. Pote, J. Hodges, J. Oswald, E. Wicksteed, J. and R. Tonson and S. Draper, J. Davidson, J. and J. Rivington, J. Ward, W. Johnston, M. Cooper, and the Executors of Mr J. Darby.
    4°: Vol. I: A^2 a–d^4 B–$3S^4$ $3T^2$; Vol. II: π^2 3V–$9F^4$ $9G^2$.   L.624.i.4.

4 Allen, J. *Synopsis medicinae.* 2nd ed. 1740.
    Vol. I of the 'third' edition of 1749 is evidently a re-issue of Vol. I.

7 *The apprentice's faithful monitor.* [1737: re-issue.]
    A copy of the 1734 edition is in ICN. Not seen.

10 Bailey, N. *An universal etymological English dictionary.* 10th ed. 1742.
    The $14\frac{1}{2}$ octavo sheets Ackers claims for were presumably 3O–$4S^4$, plus $6B^4$ (cf. the claim for the 11th ed.), not O–$4S^4$ (correspondingly, 'O' in *Ledger*, p. 160, should be '3O'). Samuel Richardson and Henry Woodfall printed parts of the 2nd ed. of 1724 (Sale, pp. 92, 147–48), and probably also of later editions.

12A —*Dictionarium Britannicum: or a more compleat universal etymological dictionary than any extant . . . Collected by several hands, the mathematical part by G. Gordon, the botanical by P. Miller. The whole revis'd and improv'd . . . by N. Bailey.* 1730. For T. Cox.
    2°: A–$Oooo^2$ 4E–$4Q^2$ $(4R)^2$ 4R–$6E^2$ ^26A–$^26E^2$ 6F–$8Q^2$ 8R1 8S1 8T1 8U1 8X–$9A^2$ 9B1 ^2A–$^2E^2$.   L.625.k.7.
    Ackers' orn. 156 is on A2 (quire A may be his only contribution).

14 —*English and Latin exercises, for school-boys: comprising all the rules of syntaxis.* 9th ed. 1734. For R. Ware.

Not seen, but MH copy (Gutman Educ. T. 20917.34) reported.

16A — *English and Latin exercises, for school-boys: comprising all the rules of syntaxis.* 12th ed. 1750. For R. Ware.

    12°: A–S⁶.   MH. Gutman Educ. T. 20917.50.

21 Bedford, A. *Animadversions upon Sir Isaac Newton's book,* [etc.]. 1728.

There are three issues with differing imprints: (i) Printed by Charles Ackers, for C. Rivington; sold by R. Knaplock, F. Fayram and J. Hooke; (ii) Printed by Charles Ackers, sold by R. Knaplock; F. Fayram; and J. Hooke; (iii) Printed by Charles Ackers, sold by R. Knaplock; and J. Hooke (Peter and Ruth Wallis, *Newton and Newtoniana 1672–1975: a bibliography*, Project for historical biobibliography, University of Newcastle upon Tyne (Folkestone, 1977), Items N315, N315.01 and N315.02; in Wallis, items 728BED28, 728BED28S and 728BED28T).

26 —*The evil and mischief of stage-playing,* [etc.]. 2nd ed. 1735.

This is a re-issue of item **31** (1730), and presumably the item debited to Wilford on 25 Nov. 1735: 'To 400 of Mr Bedford's Sermons at 4½d.' (*Ledger*, pp. 126–27).

35 Berington:

Woodhead, A. *Ancient church government, part III . . . reflecting on the . . . writings of . . . Bp. Bramhall, Dr. Potter . . . and others . . . To which is prefix'd, a preface, giving a succinct account of his writings and life* [by Simon Berington]. Printed in the year 1736.

    4°: A⁴ a–l⁴ B–2G⁴.   L.491.g.13.

Presumably, despite noted discrepancies, this is the item concerned (Foxon, Review). Contains no CA orns.

37A Biggs, W. *The military history of Europe, &c. from the commencement of the war with Spain in 1739, to the Treaty of Aix-la-Chapelle in 1748.* 1755. For R. Baldwin, J. Marshall, P. Davey and B. Law.

    8°: [A]⁴ B–U⁸ ⋆X⁸ ⋆Y⁴ ⋆Z² X–2D⁸ 2E².   L.804.d.34.

Two CA orns. appear on B1, another printer's on X1.

39 Boreman, T. *A description of three hundred animals.* 5th ed. 1743. For R. Ware.

Not seen, but NIC copy (History of Science Collections: QL. 41. B73. 1743) reported.

39A Boulainvilliers, H. de *The life of Mahomet.* Translated from the French. 1731. For W. Hinchliffe.

    8°: A⁴ a⁴ B–3D⁴.   L.10605.b.21.

Advertised in the *Grub-street journal* of 10 June 1731 as printed and sold by S. Palmer and J. Huggonson, but the presence within a⁴ of 3 orns. already in Ackers' stock suggests he supplied this half-sheet.

39B [Bowyer, W.] *A dissertation: in which the objections of a late pamphlet to the writings of the antients, after the manner of Mr. Markland, are clearly answer'd; those passages in Tully corrected, on*

*which some of the objections are founded: with amendments of a few pieces of criticism in Mr.
Markland's Epist. Critica.* 1746. For M. Cooper. Price 1s. (t.p.).

    8°: π1 A–G⁴ H1.   C.Ddd.25.101⁴.

Not in the Ledger. Three CA orns. The L catalogue identifies William Bowyer the younger
as the author, and the pamphlet as: John Ross, Bishop of Exeter, *A dissertation in which the
defence of P. Sulla, ascribed to M. Tullius Cicero, is clearly proved to be spurious* [1745].

40 Boyer, A. *Le dictionnaire royal. . . . The royal dictionary.* [Another ed.] 1748.
    L pressmark is now: 1502/396.

[Browne, Moses]: see under **226A** 'Immerito'.

48 Castle Society: see entry for **312** Musical Society.

49 Castlemaine. *An act,* [etc.].
    L pressmark is now: BS. Ref. 2/8.

50 *A catechetical instruction: being an account of,* [etc.].
    NB correct wording of title, and pressmark: L. 3504.de.10(1).

55 Chambers, E. *Cyclopaedia.* 2 vols. 5th ed. 1741–43.
    Ackers' orn. 84 is on 12B2ᵛ of Vol. II, at the end of the section for the letter T (which
begins on 12A1).

57 Christ's Hospital: List of the Governors.
    Another undated list is at O. Pamph. 313(2).

60 Chubb, T. *A discourse concerning reason, with regard to religion and divine revelation.* 2nd ed.
1746. For T. Cox.
    8°: A–G⁴ H².   ZCU (Rare Books Coll'n).
    Within *A collection of tracts, on various subjects* (1743), Vol. II, Part i.

62A —*An enquiry concerning the grounds and reasons, or what those principles are, on which two of
our anniversary solemnities are founded: viz. that on the 30th of January . . . and that on the 5th of
November . . . To which is added, the sufficiency of reason in matters of religion, farther considered.*
1732. For T. Cox. Price 1s. (t.p.).
    8°: [A]² B–K⁴.   L.699.d.16(5).
    Not in the Ledger, no orns. present, but in typographical style it closely resembles Ackers'
known work for Chubb, and the word 'ENQUIRY' on the titlepage is of the same font, and
almost certainly some of the same sorts (cp. the 'Q'), as used for the same word on [A]3 of *Four
tracts* (1734), item **65**. Bound within *A collection . . .* (1743), II, i (as for **60**).

78A Connock, R. *A collection of the names of all the princes of this kingdom of England,* [etc.]
Printed in the year 1747.
    8°: A² B–K⁴.   L.806.d.12.
    Not in the Ledger, but contains 6 CA orns. In L copy, MS note 'Publishd by J. T. Philipps'.

78B Cook, J. *An anatomical and mechanical essay on the whole animal oeconomy; in one view.* 2
vols. 1730. For W. Meadows.
    8°: Vol. II: A⁸ (–A8?) B–2A⁸ 2B⁴.   L.549.e.26,27.
    Another printer's (Woodfall's?) orns. are in Vol. I, and the first half of Vol. II. Ackers'
orns., and lighter inking, can be seen in the remaining 12½ sheets, from sheet O onwards.

78C — *Clavis naturae: or, the mystery of philosophy unvail'd.* 1733. Printed by C. Ackers, for W. Meadows, T. Astley, T. Worral.

    8°: A⁸ a² B–2C⁸ 2D⁴.   L.536.g.22.

    Not in the Ledger. Publication noticed, *LM*, Dec. 1732.

79 Cooke, T. *The comedian, or philosophical enquirer.* 1732–33.

    Not Ackers' work. See Appendix II, item **131**. Some of the orns. in it would come into Ackers' stock later.

83 Cordier, M. *Corderii colloquiorum centuria selecta.* 12th ed. 1746.

    L pressmark is now: 1568/3694.

83A — *Corderii colloquiorum centuria selecta.* 13th ed. 1749. For C. Hitch; and W. Johnston.

    12°: A⁶ B–H¹².   O.Vet. A4 f. 1940.

    Three CA orns.

84/95A Downame, J. *A brief concordance or table to the Bible of the last translation: serving for the more easy finding out of the most useful places therein contained.* 1739. For R. Ware.

    4°: A–I⁴.   O. Bib. Eng. 1744. d. 1(2).

    The presence of orn. 168 on A1ᵛ, together with the correct number of sheets being involved (nine), confirm that this is the concordance to which Ackers' entry of 16 May 1739 refers (*Ledger*, pp. 100, 116, 248).

97 Duck, S. *Poems on several subjects.* 9th ed. 1733. For J. Roberts; sold by T. Astley.

    8°: [A]⁴ B–D⁴.   CtY.Ik.D858.730j.

    Not seen, but CtY (Sterling Memorial Library) copy reported. Distinguished from other editions of the '9th edition' by its press-figures (Foxon, Vol. 1, pp. 200–201).

    [Duncombe, W.?]: see under: **337D** 'Philanthropos'.

99 Dyche, T. *A guide to the English tongue.* 20th ed. 1734. For Richard Ware.

    12°: A–F¹².   L.1607/5015(1).

110 — *A guide to the English tongue.* 27th ed. 1741. For Richard Ware.

    Professor T. W. Baldwin's copy is now in the Library of the University of Illinois (Baldwin 295). Not seen, but reported.

111 — *A guide to the English tongue.* 28th ed. 1742. For Richard Ware.

    Not seen, but BN copy reported.

130A — *A guide to the English tongue.* 37th ed. 1749. For Richard Ware.

    12°: A–F¹² G⁶.   L.1488.de.35.

    Contains 7 CA orns.

135 — *A new general English dictionary.* 5th ed. 1748.

    While the absence of orns. or other identifiers means that subsequent editions cannot be assigned to Ackers, their typographical similarity to the 5th edition makes it plausible. The relevant editions are the 6th (1750), 7th (1752), 8th (1754) and 9th (1758). Such a large book (8°: A–3L⁸), densely printed in small type, would have pre-empted quite a bit of his capacity.

136 — *The spelling dictionary: or, a collection of all the common words and proper names of persons and places, made use of in the English tongue.* 4th ed. 1737. For Richard Ware.

12⁰: A–K¹².   ZWTU.REng.DYCH.Spel.1737.

137 — *The spelling dictionary,* [etc.]. 5th ed. 1743. For R. Ware.

12⁰: A–K¹².   O.Vet. A4 f. 1938.

140 — *Vocabularium Latiale: or, a Latin vocabulary.* 7th ed. 1743. For J. Brotherton, R. Ware, S. Birt.

8⁰: [A]² B–P⁴ Q².   L.1578/8801.

Ledger: 23 Nov. 1742.

141 — *Youth's guide to the Latin tongue.* 2nd ed. 1735. For A. Bettesworth and C. Hitch, R. Ware, S. Birt, J. Hodges.

Not seen, but CLU-C copy reported.

144 *Electa majora ex Ovidio, Tibullo, et Propertio: cum consolatione ad Liviam . . . Quarto castigata,* [etc.]. 1738. Impensis A. Bettesworth & C. Hitch; G. Innys & R. Manby; J. Wood; & J. Pote, Eton.

8⁰: A⁴ B–O⁸ P⁴.   C.7700.d.696(1).

146A Ellis, W. *The London and country brewer.* 6th ed. 1750. For T. Astley; and sold by R. Baldwin.

8⁰: [A]⁴ B–Q⁸ R⁴ S–Y⁸ Z⁴ 2[A]1.   L.1400.c.22.

CA's orns. appear in Parts I and II only (i.e., to L8ᵛ), another printer's in Part III and the supplement. The 7th ed. (1759) contains orns. of another printer.

147, 149 — *The practical farmer.* 1742. For T. Astley. [Part I: 4th ed., 1742; Part II: 3rd ed., 1742.]

Not seen, but NN copy reported.

148 —*The practical farmer.* [Part II: 2nd ed., 1741. For T. Ashley (sic).]

Not seen, but NIC (Albert R. Mann Library) copy (S. 50g. E47) reported. Part I in this copy is 3rd ed., 1738.

151 Elliston, R. *Officia sacrata: or, devotional offices in the retired acts of divine adoration.* 1742.

Not seen, but NN copy (★KC1742) reported.

154 *Englishmen's eyes open'd . . . being the excise controversy set in a new light.* 1733.

'Mr. Postlethwyte', to whom the printing is debited, is possibly the author (?Malachy Postlethwayt) (Foxon, Review).

154A Entick, J. *The pocket companion and history of free-masons.* 1754. For J. Scott, sold by R. Baldwin.

12⁰: A⁴ B–O¹² P⁸.   L.1486.aa.26.

Contains 16 known CA orns., plus 3 others (also presumably his). The 2nd ed. (1759) contains orns. not known as Ackers'.

161 [Fowke, M.] *The platonick lovers.* 1732.

12⁰: A¹² (±A1) χ² B–F¹² G¹² (±G3) H¹² I⁶ (±I3.4).

Correct collation gives 'the six leaves necessary for a duodecimo half-sheet' (Foxon, Review).

164 Garth, S. *A compleat key to the dispensary.* 4th ed. 1746. For Thomas Astley. Price 6d. (t.p.).
12°: A–D⁶.   L.1607/564.

164A Gay, J. *The distress'd wife.* 2nd ed. 1750. For T. Astley.
8°: A⁴ B–F⁸.   L.643.g.10(1).
Contains 6 known CA orns., plus 2 others on the half-title.

166A *A general view of religion.* 1729. Printed for J. Roberts. Price 1s. (half-title).
8°: A⁴ B–F⁸.   C.Ddd.25.219⁴.

177 Goldsmith. *An almanack for the year of our Lord God, MDCCXLV.* [1744]. Printed by
Charles Ackers, for the Company of Stationers.
   Not seen, but copy sold in 1988 by Patrick King Ltd., of Stony Stratford, Bucks., to
McMaster University, Hamilton, Canada. Described in King's Bulletin No. 14 (1988), as
item 2.

179 —*An almanack for the year of our Lord God, MDCCXLVII.* [1746]. Printed by Charles
Ackers, for the Company of Stationers.
24°: A–B¹².   C.Syn.9.74.10.
Sheet B appears to be misbound in the C copy.

184A Gonson, J. *The charge of Sir John Gonson Knt. to the grand jury of the city and liberty of
Westminster, &c. . . .* [*24 April 1728*]. 1728. Printed by Charles Ackers.
8°: A–D⁴.   L.113.i.25.
Ackers' edition of the 'first charge'.

188 — *Three charges.* 1728.
In the notes, '28 Apr.' should read '24 Apr.'.

189, 190 — *Three charges.* 1728.
Item **189** is described on its title-page as the 2nd ed., i.e., is identical with item **190**.

207 [Halfpenny, W.] *The builder's pocket-companion.* 'By Michael Hoare'. 3rd ed. 1747. For R.
Ware.
Not seen, but PU-FA copy reported.

210 Hayes, R. *The broker's breviat.* 1734.
There is now a copy in L, shelfmark 1606/1985. Wallis 718HAY33/34.

216 — *Interest at one view, calculated to a farthing.* 4th ed. 1741. For W. Meadows.
16°: A–T⁸ U⁴.   LU.[GL]1741.
Ledger: 25 November 1740. Wallis 718HAY32/41.

218A — *Interest at one view.* 8th ed. 1751. For W. Meadows.
16°: A–Y⁸.   C.U★.8.44(G).
Three CA orns. Wallis 718HAY32/51.

218B — *Interest at one view.* 9th ed. 1754. For W. Meadows.
Not seen, but copy at Keele University Library reported. Wallis 718HAY32/54.

218C — *Interest at one view.* 10th ed. 1758. For W. Meadows.
16⁰: A–Y⁸.   LU.[GL]1732
Three CA orns. Wallis 718HAY32/58.

225A Hodgkin, W. *A short, new, and easy method of working the rule of practice in arithmetick.* 1731. Printed by C. Ackers; and sold by W. Page and T. Mount; S. Birt; T. Worrall; J. Stagg; H. Whitridge; and by the author. Price 1s. 6d. (t.p.).
8⁰: A⁴ (–A4) B–P⁴ Q1.   L.530.c.15(1).
Wallis 731HOD31.

226A 'Immerito' [Browne, Moses]. *Piscatory eclogues: an essay to introduce new rules, and new characters, into pastoral.* 1729. Printed by C. Ackers, for John Brindley. Price 2s. 6d. (t.p.).
8⁰: A⁴ b⁴ (–b4) B–R⁴ S1.   L.992.k.24(2).
Foxon B531.

229 Jeffries, D. *A treatise on diamonds and pearls.* 1750.
Correct shelfmark is LU[GL]1750.

231 Jenkin, R. *The reasonableness and certainty of the Christian religion.* 2 vols. 6th ed. 1734.
Bowyer claims for printing all of Vol. I; hence Ackers' claim for printing 19 sheets evidently refers to Vol. II, despite the statement in its imprint that it was 'Printed by T.W.' (Thomas Wood?).

235 Justin. *M. J. Justini ex Trogi Pompeii historiis externis. Libri xliv . . . To which is added, the words of Justin disposed in a grammatical or natural order,* [etc.] *by N. Bailey.* 1732. For J. Brotherton, [etc.].
8⁰: A⁴ a² b–y⁴ B–3O⁴ [3P²?].   ZAU.G.c.878.9/J96h/1732.
Ackers claimed for printing 17½ sheets. His orns. are found within quires A, y and B. ZAU copy lacks leaves 2R3, 2R4, and quire 3P (2 leaves or 4?). Copy also in MiU (not seen).

241 *Al Mesra; or Mahommed's famous night-journey to Jerusalem upon the ass Elborak, and from thence with the angel Gabriel to heaven, as mention'd in the 17th chapter of the Koran, lately publish'd. Translated . . . by . . . Mr. Wild.* 1734. Printed and sold by J. Wilford.
8⁰: [A]² B–N⁴ O².   O.Vet. A4 e. 2612.
Ackers' claim for printing one half-sheet evidently relates to the quarter-sheets [A] and O, in both of which his orns. appear. The rest of the book was probably printed by Huggonson.

241A Labelye, Charles. *The result of a particular view of the north level of the fens, taken in August, 1745.* 1748. Printed by C. and J. Ackers.
8⁰: [A]⁴ B⁴.   CCRO.R59/31.
I am grateful to Mr K. I. D. Maslen for locating this item.

241B *The ladies advocate: or, wit and beauty a match for treachery and inconstancy.* 1749. For C. Long.
12⁰: [A]⁴ B–N¹² O⁸.   L.12614.eee.13.
Two CA orns.

241C Langham, T. *The nett duties and drawbacks payable on importation and exportation of all sorts of merchandize, digested into an easy method.* 8th ed. 1758. For W. Meadows, J. Brotherton.
8⁰: A–2O⁴ 2P².   L.8245.aaa.15.
Two CA orns.

253A Locke, R. *The circle squared. To which is added, a problem to discover the longitude both at land and sea.* 1730. Printed by C. Ackers, for the author, sold at J. Shirley's and by the booksellers of London and Westminster.

    8⁰: A⁴ (–A1) B–D⁴ (D1 + χ1).   L.533.e.24(12).

    Wallis identifies 2 issues, the second with a frontispiece (730LOC30 and 730LOC30S).

254A — *A new problem to discover the longitude at sea,* [etc.]. 1751. For R. Baldwin. Price 6d. (t.p.).

    8⁰: A–C⁴.   O. 8⁰ E 89 Art.

    Two CA orns. Diagram bound in following C4.

255 [Lockman, J.] *A new history of England, by question and answer.* 2nd ed. 1735. For T. Astley.

    12⁰: A–T⁶.   O.Vet. A4 f. 1749.

    Corrects previous title. Ackers' claim for 5½ sheets evidently relates to half-sheets A–L, within which his orns. are found (hence the possibility that the Ledger entry relates to Oldmixon's *History of England* is eliminated).

270 *The London magazine.* 1745.

    An unbound copy of the Appendix with the 'original wrapper' is in C (Broughton 561). This is a two-leaf wraparound, with, on the first recto, a half-title, a summary description of the contents, and (as this is the last issue for the year) instructions for the binder. The remaining pages are filled with advertisements. From 1746 blue paper covers were introduced, probably to protect the monthly title-pages, which came into use in March.

285 *The loss of liberty,* [etc.].

    The author is identified as M. Lonsdale by a MS note in the O copy (Foxon L270–71).

288 'Lyttleton'. Substitute:

    The progress of divine love: a poem. Written by a young lady of fifteen, in the year 1731. 1732. Ledger: 14 July 1732. Advertised in the *Grub-street journal,* 18 July 1732, as 'Printed for N. Cholmondely', to whom the item is debited. No copy is known to survive (see Foxon, Review and P1108). G. Lyttleton's *Progress of love* was printed by Wright (McLaverty, p. 15).

288A *Madness: a poem. Written by a gentleman when under confinement for lunacy.* 1728. Printed; and sold by J. Roberts. Price 6d. (t.p.).

    4⁰: [A]² B–E².   L.643.k.3(6).

    One CA orn. Foxon M13.

289A *Man and woman. A dissertation on the communion of bodies, humbly inscrib'd to the publick.* 1732. For T. Cox. Price 6d. (t.p.).

    8⁰: A–D⁴.   LW.9.26.5(5).

    Five CA orns.

290 [Mann, N.] *Of the true years of the birth and of the death of Christ.* 1733.

    Correct title (not 'birth and death').

297 Mather, W. *The young man's companion: or, arithmetick made easy.* 17th ed. 1747. For R. Ware, T. Longman and T. Shewell, A. Clarke. Price 2s. 6d. (t.p.).

    Not seen, but DLC copy (AG104. M35. 1747) reported.

309 [Morris, J.] *Deliverance from public dangers, a solemn call for a national reformation, set forth in a serious and compassionate address to the inhabitants of Great Britain and Ireland*, [etc.]. 1747. Printed for the author, and sold by J. Noon and J. Buckland.

8°: A–D^4 E1.   C.Syn.7.74.27^9.

Referred to in the Ledger as 'A serious and compassionate address'.

310A Moses of Chorene (Moses Khorenaci). *Mosis Chorenensis historiae Armeniacae libri III . . . Armeniace ediderunt, Latine verterunt, notisque illustrarunt Gulielmus & Georgius, Gul. Whistoni filii.* 1736. Ex officina Caroli Ackers typographi; apud Joannem Whistonum bibliopolam.

4°: π^2 a–c^4 B–3D^4 3E–3I^2.   L.148.c.4.

Not in the Ledger.

311 Mottley, J. *The history of . . . the empress Catharine.* 1744.

L pressmark: 1056.g.11,12.

311A Musgrave, W. *Genuine memoirs of the life and character of the right honourable Sir Robert Walpole, and of the family of the Walpoles,* [etc.]. 1732. Printed for E. Curll. Price '(of the two parts)' 3s. (t.p.).

8°: A^4 a1 B–G^4 H1; ^{2}B–^{2}K^4 ^{2}L^4 (–^{2}L4); ^{3}A–^{3}B^4.   C.Ddd.25.150$^{13-14}$.

Ackers' orns. are in the preliminaries and second sequence (the first text sequence contains none; the third is Curll's catalogue).

312 Musical Society.

Clearly this is identical with the 'Castle Society': see item **48**. Cf. *The laws of the Musical Society, at the Castle-Tavern, in Pater-noster-row. Printed in the year 1751* (O. Godw. Pamph. 1859(10)), which is probably not Ackers' work. It collates 16°: A–C^4.

314 Nepos, C. *Cornelii Nepotis vitae excellentium imperatorum: cum versione anglica . . . or, Cornelius Nepos's Lives of the excellent commanders, with an English translation . . . by John Clarke.* 6th ed. 1742. For J. Clarke, C. Hitch.

Not seen, but CtY (Beinecke Rare Book & MS Library) copy (1974. 2290) reported.

314A — *Cornelii Nepotis vitae excellentium imperatorum . . . with an English translation . . . By John Clarke.* 7th ed. 1748. For C. Hitch, W. Johnston.

8°: A–Mm^4.   CtY.Gnn40.g722g.

Not seen, but CtY (Sterling Memorial Library) copy reported.

316A [Newton, W.] *The life of the right reverend Dr. White Kennett, late Lord Bishop of Peterborough.* 1730. For S. Billingsley; and sold by J. Roberts; and T. Cox.

8°: A^8 a^2 B–T^8 U1.   C.Rel.f.7b.5.

Another issue has '. . . for S. Billingsley' (C. Peterborough V.2.43). In pencil on its title-page is 'by Rev Robt Newton. V. of Gillingham Dorset'. The L catalogue gives his name as 'William'. A third issue has 'For T. Cox; J. Brindley; F. Cogan; and J. Stag' (L.276.h.46).

321A *The opposition. To be published occasionally.* 1755. Sold by M. Cooper.

8°: [A^4] B–C^4 D^2.   O. G. Pamph. 1175(9) and (12).

Apparently only one 'issue' was published.

324 Ovid. *Minellius Anglicanus, sive Publii Ovidii Nasonis metamorphosewm* [sic] *libri xv. Una cum argumentis cujusque fabulae, notisque Minellianus anglice redditis opera & studio N. Bailey.* 2nd ed. 1733. Typis H. Barker.

Perhaps the 'Bailey's Ovid' for which Ackers claimed for contributing $5\frac{1}{2}$ sheets on 1 June 1732. Not seen, but there are copies at MH, MB. Alternatively it may have been an edition of Bailey's text of the *Epistolae heroides*.

324A — *De tristibus libri v. Interpretatione & notis illustravit Daniel Crispinus,* [etc.]. 4th ed. 1750. Typis Caroli & Johannis Ackers, impensis Societatis Stationariorum.

    8°: A–L⁸ M–R⁴ S1.   L.1001.h.22.

330 Pascal, B. *Thoughts on religion.* 4th ed. 1741.

Re-issued with a new title-page, again as the 4th ed., in 1749 (O. Vet. A4 e. 917).

335 Petis de la Croix, F. *The Persian and Turkish tales, compleat.* 2 vols. 4th ed. 1739. For Richard Ware. Price 6s. (t.p.).

    12°: Vol. I: A⁶ B–T¹² U²; Vol. II: A⁶ B–R¹² S¹² (–S6,7).   L.1507/1041.

A leaflet advertising the publication of this edition is in Joseph Ames's Collection of title-pages and fragments in L (Ames. 6, item 3030).

337A Phaedrus. *Phaedri fabulae: or, Phaedrus's fables, with the following improvements; in a method intirely new . . . For the use of schools. By John Stirling.* 5th ed. 1750. For T. Astley, sold by R. Baldwin, jun.

    8°: π1 A⁸ (–A8) B–L⁸ M⁴ [N]1.   L.1578/37.

337B — *Phaedri fabulae: or, Phaedrus's fables,* [etc.]. 6th ed. 1755. For Thomas Astley, sold by R. Baldwin.

    8°: A⁸ (–A8) B–L⁸ M⁴.   L.1578/26.

337C 'Philalethes'. *A free and impartial enquiry into the reasons of the present extravagant price of coals.* 1729. For T. Cox. Price 6d. (t.p.).

    8°: A–E⁴.   LU.[GL]1729.

Three CA orns.

337D 'Philanthropos' [Duncombe, William?] *A letter to Mr. Law; occasion'd by reading his Treatise on Christian perfection: with a copy of verses, address'd to the same author. By a lover of mankind.* 1728. Printed for W. Hinchliffe. Price 6d. (t.p.).

    8°: A–E⁴.   C.Ddd.25.219³.

Dedicatory epistle signed 'Philanthropos'. Handwritten note in C copy ascribes to Duncombe.

339 Philipps, J. T. *Dissertationes historicae quatuor.* 1735.

Correct collation: 8°: A⁴ (+erratum slip on A1ᵛ) B–Nn⁴ Oo⁴ (–Oo4).

346 *The philosophical transactions (from the year 1719, to the year 1733) abridged, and disposed under general heads. By John Eames and John Martyn.* 2 vols. [Vols. VI, VII]. 1734. For J. Brotherton, J. Hazard, W. Meadows, T. Cox, W. Hinchliffe, W. Bickerton, T. Astley, S. Austen, L. Gilliver, and R. Willock.

Vols. VI and VII of *The philosophical transactions and collections . . . abridged and disposed under general heads,* 11 vols., 1716–56. Note correct titles, and L pressmark: 462.f.1–11. (Vols. VI and VII: 462.f.6, 7).

348 Pine, J. *A proposal by John Rocque, surveyor, and John Pine, engraver, for engraving and printing, by subscription, a new, accurate and comprehensive plan of the cities of London and Westminster, and borough of Southwark,* [etc.]. Subscriptions are to be taken in by John Pine . . . and by John Rocque. [1740.]

Ledger 18 June 1740. Not seen, but copy in Chetham's Library, Manchester, reproduced as a frontispiece to *The A to Z of Georgian London*, with introductory notes by Ralph Hyde, London Topographical Society publication no. 126, (London, 1982). Half-sheet folio.

350 — *A proposal,* [etc.]. [2nd ed.]. 1740.

Ledger 28 Oct. 1740. Not seen, but copies in MH, CtY. At head, 'October 24, 1740'. Half-sheet folio.

353A Pledger, Elias. *A brief description of a new invented, small, yet accurate astronomical quadrant.* 1731. For W. Meadows. Price 2s. (t.p.).

    8⁰: A⁴ (–A4?) B–K⁴ [I]1.   C. White c.62.

Two large, folded leaves bound in following E4, [I]1.

354 Poisson de Gomez, M. A. *La belle assemblée: being a curious collection of some very remarkable incidents which happen'd to persons of the first quality in France.* 4 vols. 5th ed. 1743. For D. Browne, J. Brotherton, W. Meadows, R. Ware, H. Lintot, T. Cox, T. Astley, S. Austen, J. Hodges, and E. Comins.

    12⁰: Vol. IV: [A]1 B–P¹².   L.1578/5282.

Ackers printed Vol. IV only.

355 — *La belle assemblée,* [etc.]. 4 vols. 6th ed. 1749. For D. Browne, J. Brotherton, W. Meadows, R. Ware, H. Lintot, T. Cox, T. Astley, S. Austen, J. Hodges, and E. Comins.

    12⁰: Vol. IV: A1 B–P¹².   L.1578/3622.

This is doubtless the edition for which Ackers records printing the 14 sheets of the fourth volume in 1747. Contains his orns.

365A Price, F. *A treatise on carpentry.* 1733. Printed by C. Ackers, for the author; and sold by W. Meadows; T. Astley; and T. Worrall. Price 5s. stitched (t.p.).

    4⁰: A–B⁴ (–B4) C–E⁴ F².   O.Don. d. 191.

The printing of this item is not claimed for in the Ledger, but Ackers sold copies on 23 May 1733 to Messrs. Finch and Barrit (publication advertised in *LM*, May 1733). Wallis 733PRI33.

369A *A proposal for the better regulation of the stage.* 1732. For J. Peele. Price 1s. (t.p.).

    8⁰: A–H⁴.   L.641.e.28(5).

Not in the Ledger. Contains 8 CA orns.

373A Psalms: *The whole book of Psalms.* 1748. Printed by C. and J. Ackers, for the Company of Stationers.

Not seen, but copies in MB, MiU, NIC.

376A — *The whole book of Psalms.* 1754. Printed by C. and J. Ackers, for the Company of Stationers.

    8⁰: A–H⁴.   ZDU.Eb.1754.B.

Not seen, but Otago University copy reported by K. I. D. Maslen.

383 Ralph, J. *Miscellaneous poems, by several hands.* 1729.
12°: A⁶ B–P¹² Q⁶.
Note correct collation, and L pressmark: 992.b.30.

384 — *Miscellaneous poems.* 1729.
The various poems can be found issued separately:
Night. 2nd ed. 1729: L. 992.k.15(1).
Zeuma. 1729: not seen, but copies at DLC, CtY, MB, MH.
Clarinda. 1729: O.Vet. A4 e. 763.
The muses' address to the king. 1728: O.G. Pamph. 1286(2).

385 — *Night: a poem.* 1728.
8°: A–E⁸ F⁸ (–F7,8).
Corrects previous collation (Foxon, Review).

387 *The reformation reformed,* [etc.]. 1743. For T. Cox.
8°: A–G⁴ H². CtY.Beinecke Mhc7.A14.
Not seen, but CtY (Beinecke Rare Book & MS Library) copy reported.

388 [Reynolds, G.] *A dissertation,* [etc.]. 1732.
A copy of the '2nd ed.' is at L.689.b.22(1).

388A Robinson, N. *A discourse upon the nature and cause of sudden deaths; and the reason why such numbers of people died suddenly in the years 1730 and 1731.* 1732. For T. Warner. Price 1s. 6d. (t.p.).
8°: π1 A–M⁴ N². L.1038.l.27.
Not in the Ledger. Contains 13 CA orns.

389A [St. John, Henry, Viscount Bolingbroke]. *The monumental inscription on the column at Blenheim-House erected to the immortal memory of the late Duke of Marlborough.* 1731. For W. Hinchliffe. Price 6d. (t.p.).
2°: [A]² B². L.599.k.19(7).
Contains one CA orn.

390 Sallust. *C. Sallustii Crispi bellum Catilinarium, et Jugurthinum, ad ultimam Wassii editionem diligenter castigata, cum commentariis Johannis Min-ellii.* [2nd ed. 1738. Impensis Societatis Stationariorum.]
Not seen or located. Title from 1st ed., 12°, Oxford, 1730, copy in O (23642 f. 4).

391A Sedgwick:
Ledger: 30 Jan. 1733–4; his 'Case' may be a reprint of *The case of John Sedgwick, Gent.*, 1731 (L.515.l.15(16)), although the L catalogue describes it as one sheet folio and the Ledger refers to a half-sheet. Not seen.

395A Shelley, G. *Sentences and maxims divine, moral, and historical, in prose and verse.* 3rd ed. 1752. Printed by C. and J. Ackers, for S. and E. Ballard.
16°: A⁴ B–I⁸ K². L.722.c.8.

396 *A short letter to the letter-writer concerning the duties on wines and tobacco.* 1733.
Sedgwick, to whom the printing is debited, may be the author (Foxon, Review).

400A Slade, John. *Love and duty. A tragedy.* 1756. For R. Griffiths.
    8⁰: A–H⁴ I². C.S721.d.70.35⁸.

405 Stanislaus: *The history of Stanislaus I*, [etc.]. 1741.
    The author is Philippe de Cantillon.

406 [Stephens, W.] *A journal of the proceedings in Georgia, beginning October 20, 1737.* 3 vols. 1742.
    Vol. III not seen, but E copy (137.b.g) reported. Cf. J. C. Ross, 'Charles Ackers and William Stephens' *Journal*', *Georgia historical quarterly*, 52 (1968), 434–37.

407 — *A journal received February 4, 1741, by the Trustees . . . from William Stephens.* 1742. For W. Meadows.
    Not seen, but MiU–C copy reported. This is a re-imposition of $2\frac{3}{4}$ sheets of item **406**, Vol. III.

408 — *A state of the province of Georgia*, [etc.]. 1742.
    8⁰: [A]² B–E⁴.
    Note correct collation.

409 [Stretzer, T.] *The natural history*, [etc.]. 1732.
    Not Ackers' work. The supposition in the original note to item **3** (Albin) is presumably correct (Foxon, Review).

411 Switzer, S. *The practical husbandman and planter*, [etc.]. 2 vols. 1733–4.
    Vol. II: 8⁰: a⁴ B⁴ c–f⁴; (July) *A*⁴ (–*A*4) [a]–[c]⁴ [e]² B–2E⁴; (August) A⁴ (–*A*4) a–d⁴ B–2C⁴; (September) *A*⁴ (–*A*4) b–d⁴ e⁴ (-e4) B–U⁴ X². L.1609/4807.
    Ackers claims on 1 May 1734 for printing the August section only, but his orns. also appear in the preliminaries to the July issue. (I am grateful to Mr R. Goulden of the British Library for supplying this collation. As the printer uses square brackets, italic has been introduced to identify inferred signing.)

415 Thomson, G. *The anatomy of the human bones.* 1734.
    The title-page in the O copy (Vet. A4 e. 2718) is stated in the O catalogue to be a cancel.

417 Tull, J. *The horse-hoing husbandry*, [etc.]. 1733.
    The 'second edition' of 1743, printed for A. Millar, described as 'compleat in four parts', is a re-issue of the body of the book with a cancel title-page and the 'second edition' of the supplement, dated 1740 (in LU, pressmark [GL] 1743 fol.). The first edition of the supplement, not in the L copy of item **417** described, but present in the LU copy (pressmark [GL] 1733 fol.), is dated 1736 and collates, as does the 2nd: [3F]1 3G–3T²; 2[A]1 ²B–²D²; ³A–³B².

419A Turner, W. *Exercises to the accidence and grammar: or, an exemplification of the several moods and tenses, and of the principal rules of construction*, [etc.]. 8th ed. 1752. For S. and E. Ballard; and T. Longman.
    12⁰: A⁶ (–A6?) B–Y⁶ Z1. O.Vet. A5 f. 2379.

420 Twells, L. *The theological works of the learned Dr. Pocock.* 1740.
    Professor Peter Dixon (review, *N & Q*, 18 (1971), 75–76) has drawn attention to letters from Twells to Thomas Rawlins, reprinted in Percy Simpson, *Proof-reading in the sixteenth, seventeenth and eighteenth centuries* (Oxford, 1935), pp. 145–47, which show that our suggestion

that 'Printing of the first volume was probably completed by mid-1738' is not correct. On 27 January 1739 Twells wrote that 'all is printed except the Indexes and about half of ye Life'; the latter is the first section of Vol. I.

420A Underhill, E. *Celsus triumphatus: or, Moses vindicated.* 1732. For W. Meadows. Price 1s. (t.p.).
    8°: A–F⁴.   C.Syn.7.73.389⁹.

421 *The universal pocket companion,* [etc.]. 1741.
    The author is John Hewitt (L.12209.c.1).

421A Uvedale, T. *A cure for love: a satyr.* 2nd ed. 1732. For T. Warner. Price 1s. (t.p.).
    4°: A² a⁴ B–G⁴ H².   O.G. Pamph. 1287(8).
    Contains 6 CA orns. Foxon U34.

421B Vallensius, J. *Bibliotheca Vallensiana: or, a catalogue of the library of Jacob Vallensius . . . which will be sold the 23rd day of this instant April, 1729 . . . at the shop of Abraham Vandenhoeck.* 1729. [Colophon: Printed by C. Ackers.]
    12°: [A]² B–O⁴.   L.820.c.7(1).

421C Vandenhoeck, A. *Catalogus librorum . . . or, a catalogue of the most rare and uncommon books . . . which will be sold . . . the 12th of January 1730.* 1730. Printed by C. Ackers, for Abram. Vandenhoeck.
    8°: π1 A–K⁴ L⁴ (–L4).   L.S.C.378(3).

422A *A view of the depredations and ravages committed by the Spaniards on the British trade and navigation.* 1731. For W. Hinchliffe. Price 1s. (t.p.).
    8°: A⁴ a² B–F⁴ G².   L.114.l.47.
    Four CA orns.

423A Virgil. *The works of Virgil: translated into English blank verse. With large explanatory notes, and critical observations. By Joseph Trapp.* 3 vols. 4th ed. 1755. For W. Meadows, S. Birt.
    12°: Vol. III: [A]1 B–T¹².   L.1578/2820.
    Vols. I and II contain orns. of other printer(s).

425 Warburton, J. *Vallum romanum.*
    A specimen of the first two leaves of text, annotated, with drafts of a letter to MPs soliciting subscriptions, of two advertisements, and of most of the preface, are in Joseph Ames' collection of materials relating to printing, British Library, MS Add. 5151.

431 Wase, C. *Methodi practicae specimen; an essay of a practical grammar; or, an enquiry after a more easy and certain help to the construing and parsing of authors and to the making and speaking of Latin.* 16th ed. 1745.
    Not seen, but RPB copy reported.

436 Winslow, J. *An anatomical exposition of the structure of the human body. Translated from the French original, by G. Douglas, M.D.* 2 vols. 2nd ed. 1743. For R. Ware, J. and P. Knapton, S. Birt, T. Longman, C. Hitch, C. Davis, and T. Astley.
    4°: Vol. I: A⁴ a–b⁴ B–2U⁴ (–2U4); Vol. II: π1 (= 2U4) A⁴ A–2Z⁴ 3A².   L.1601/1.

436A — *An anatomical exposition of the structure of the human body*. 4th ed. 1756. For R. Ware, J. Knapton, S. Birt, T. and T. Longman, C. Hitch and L. Hawes, C. Davis, T. Astley, and R. Baldwin.

    4°: Vol. I: A^4 a–b^4 B–2U^4 (–2U4); Vol. II: π1 (=2U4) A^4 A–2Z^4 3A^2.   O.165 h. 15. CA's orns. are in Vol. II only.

441A Young, E. *The revenge, a tragedy*. [Another edition.] 1754. For D. Browne, C. Hitch and L. Hawes; J. Hodges; J. and J. Rivington; and J. Jackson.

    12°: A–C^{12}.   ZAU.G.c.822.508/E58,v.8.

Bound in *The British theatre*, '1750', For T. Lownds, Vol. 8.

Preliminary Check-list of Books Printed by Samuel Palmer

THE following list provides short titles for books that have been identified as coming from Samuel Palmer's printing-house between 1717 and 1732, either by their imprints, or from the evidence of ornaments known to have been already in his possession. Anonymous works are listed by title. For 1729–32 a number of books and ornaments relate to his partnership with John Huggonson, including some issued in 1732 subsequent to his death in May. As in previous sections, the place of publication (London) has been omitted, and digraphs expanded.

1717

1 'Democri-Diogenes' [Bockett, Elias?]. *Γιβσωνογραφία: or the picture*. Printed in the year 1717. L.G.13782(1).

2 [Nevil, Henry]. *The first of August, the anniversary of his majesty's happy accession to the throne of his ancestors. A poem*. [Anr. ed.] 1717. Printed by S. Palmer, for the author.
Not seen, but copy in CLU-C (Foxon N41).

3 [—?] *On the nativity of our blessed lord and saviour Jesus Christ. A divine poem*. 1717. Printed by S. Palmer, for the author. L.11631.e.76.
Foxon O213; cf. re-issue, 1718, O214.

4 [—] *A poem on the birth-day of . . . King George*. 1717. Printed by S. Palmer, for the author.
L.643.l.24(33★).
Foxon N49.

1718

5 Coles, Elisha. *A practical discourse of God's soveraignty*. 7th ed. 1718. Printed by S. Palmer, for J. and B. Sprint, A. Bell, S. Burrows, T. Cox, and J. Batley. L.4256.aa.18.

6 E., R. *Exchange no robbery: or, a fair equivalent for the test*. 1718. Printed by S. Palmer for R. Cruttenden and T. Cox. L.116.d.44.

7 Grove, Henry. *An essay towards a demonstration of the soul's immateriality*. 1718. For John Clark. C.Syn.5.71.18[8].

8 [Nevil, Henry]. *A poem on the anniversary of his majesty's birth-day.* Printed for the author in the year 1718.   L.643.l.24(39★).

Foxon N45.

9 Ovid. *P. Ovidii Nasonis Metamorphosis, ex accuratissimis virorum doctissimorum castigationibus emendata, & in lucem edita.* 1718. Excudebat S. Palmer, pro Societate Stationariorum.

Not seen, title-page in Ames Collection of title-pages and fragments (L. Ames. 6, item 2440). Cf. no. **120**.

10 *Reflections upon some errors in the doctrine of protestants and papists, concerning divine predestination and the points therewith connex'd,* [etc.]. 1718. Printed, and sold by J. Roberts, J. Harrison, and J. Whitworth (Manchester).   C.8.36.42⁹.

11 Rous, Francis. *The great oracle: or, the main frame and body of the scriptures, resolving the question, whether in man's free-will and common grace, or in God's special and effectual grace, stands the safety of man, and the glory of God by man's safety?* 1718. Printed by S. Palmer for John Clark.

L.3149.de.37.

12 Trail(e), Robert. *A steadfast adherence to the profession of our faith, recommended in several sermons.* 1718. For R. Cruttenden.   L.4460.aaa.21.

1719

13 Burnett, G. *The son's equality with the father prov'd from his being the object of religious worship.* 1719. For John Clark.   C.8.36.41⁹.

14 *The doctrine of the blessed trinity stated & defended.* By some London ministers. 1719. For J. Clark: and E. Matthews.   C.9.43.72¹¹.

15 Evans, John. *A letter to Mr. Cumming.* 1719. For John Clark, and Em. Matthews.

C.Syn.7.71.67¹³.

16 Ovid. P. Ovidii Nasonis. *Heroidum epistolae,*
   III Amorum
   III De arte amandi ⎫ *libri.*
   II De remedio amoris ⎭
[etc.]. 1719. Ex officina Palmeriana pro Societate Stationariorum.   ZAP.RBR.1719.Ovid.

17 Peirce, James. *The case of the ministers ejected at Exon.* 1719. For John Clark.

C.Syn.5.71.67¹⁵.

18 [Saunders, Samuel]. *A letter to the reverend Mr. Tong, Mr. Robinson, Mr. Smith, & Mr. Reynolds.* By a layman. 2nd ed. 1719. For John Clark.   C.9.43.72¹².

19 *A true relation of some proceedings at Salters-Hall . . . March 3. 1719.* 1719. For John Clark; and E. Matthews.   C.9.43.72³.

20 Watts, Isaac. *The psalms of David, imitated,* [etc.]. 2nd ed. 1719. For J. Clark; R. Ford; and R. Cruttenden.   L.3435.aaa.36.

21 [Allestree, Richard?]. *The whole duty of man, laid down in a plain and familiar way, for the use of all*, [etc.]. 1720. [Printed by S. Palmer] For J. Basket.   L.852.d.28.

22 *A calculation of the new scheme for the disposing of the South-Sea property.* [1720]. Printed by S. Palmer for J. Roberts, A. Dodd, T. Griffith, and J. Billingsley.   L.8245.g.4(37).
   The L catalogue dates this '[1721?]'. Another issue is 'for J. Roberts', see Wallis 720αCA20.

23 Crowe, William. *Oratio in martyrium regis Caroli I.* 1720. Typis S. Palmer, impensis B. Lintot.   L.731.i.31(4).

24 De Laune, Thomas. *A plea for the non-conformists.* 1720. For John Marshall.
                                      C.Pam.6.83.11[11].

25 Henley, John. *The compleat linguist.* Nos. 6–10. 1720–26. For J. Roberts, J. Pemberton.
   No. 6: *A grammar of the Hebrew tongue.* March–May 1720.
   No. 7: *A grammar of the Chaldee tongue.* 1721.
   No. 8: *A grammar of the Arabic tongue.* 1722.
   No. 9: *A grammar of the Syriac tongue.* 1723.
   No. 10: *An introduction to an English grammar.* 1726. Printed, and sold by J. Roberts; J. Woodman; J. Stone; and R. King.
   The evidence of orns. suggests Palmer was not the printer of Nos. 1–5, issued in 1719–20. They contain a variant of a known headpiece, and an unknown factotum. Copy seen: Scolar Press facsimile edition, reproducing nos. 1–9 from copy in Reading University Library, no. 10 from a L exemplar (626.g.9(1)).

26 Mitchell, Joseph. *Jonah: a poem.* 1720. Printed by S. Palmer, for J. Roberts, and A. Dodd.
                                      L.11631.c.31.
   Foxon M309; cf. fine-paper issue, M310 (in O), and 2nd edn., M311, same imprint (copy in E).

27 Nepos, Cornelius. *Cornelius Nepos de Vitis excellentium imperatorum. Interpretatione & notis illustravit Nicolaus Courtin.* 4th ed. 1720. Ex typographeio S. Palmer, & prostant venales apud J. & B. Sprint; et D. Midwinter.   C.Ely d.369.

28 [Raleigh, Walter]. *Sir Walter Raleigh's observations on the British fishery, . . . address'd and presented to King James I.* 1720. Reprinted in the year 1720. And sold by J. Roberts.
                                      C.Pryme d.384.

29 *The yea and nay stock-jobbers, or the 'Change-Alley Quakers anatomiz'd.* 1720. For J. Roberts, A. Dodd and J. Billingsly.   L.G.13782(3).
   Foxon B308. The author, 'Damon', is probably Elias Bockett.

30 Beveridge, William. *Institutionum chronologicarum libri duo.* 3rd ed. 1721. Ex officinâ Sam. Palmer, impensis J. Knapton.   L.1608/2142.

31 [Gildon, Charles]. *The laws of poetry, as laid down by the Duke of Buckinghamshire in his Essay* *on poetry, by the Earl of Roscommon in his Essay on translated verse, and by the Lord Lansdowne on Unnatural flights in poetry, explain'd and illustrated.* 1721. For J. Morley.   L.1087.c.7.

Known Palmer orns. appear in the last sheet only. Another issue was printed 'For W. Hinchliffe; and J. Walthoe' (copy at C. 7720.d.1292).

32 *The Independent Whig.* 1721. For J. Peele.   C. Acton c. 25. 391.

SP's orn. is on t.p., but rest of book has unknown orns.

33 Ramsay, Allan. *Robert, Richy and Sandy. A pastoral on the death of Matthew Prior.* 1721. Printed by S. Palmer, for Bernard Lintot, sold by J. Roberts.   L.11631.d.44. Foxon R88.

1722

34 [Bockett, Elias]. *All the wonders of the world out-wonderd* [sic]: *in the amazing and incredible prophecies of Ferdinando Albumazarides.* 1722. For J. Smith, and sold by the booksellers of London and Westminster.   L.G.13782(4).

35 Cassiodorus Senator, Flaurus Magnus Aurelius. *Cassiodorii Senatoris Complexiones in epistolas acta apostolorum & apocalypsin . . . opera & cura Samuelis Chandleri.* 1722. Typis Samuelis Palmer. Prostant venales apud Joann. Morley.   L.852.b.17.

36 Ditton, Humphrey. *A discourse concerning the resurrection of Jesus Christ.* 1722. Printed by S. Palmer, for J. Batley; and T. Cox.   L.1019.m.7.

37 Gibson, William. *The farrier's new guide.* 3rd ed. Printed by S. Palmer, for William Taylor. Not seen, copy in IU.

38 Gordon, Patrick. *Geography anatomiz'd: or, the geographical grammar.* 9th ed. 1722. Printed by S. Palmer, for R. Knaplock, J. and B. Sprint, S. Burroughs, D. Midwinter, A. Bettesworth, R. Ford, A. Ward, and J. Clark.   L.571.c.35.

39 Juvenal & Persius. *D. Junii Juvenalis et A. Persii Flacci Satirae. Interpretatione ac notis illustravit Ludovicus Prateus,* [etc.]. 1722. Typis Sam. Palmer, impensis J. & B. Sprint, R. Wilkin, B. Tooke, D. Midwinter, A. Bettesworth, [and 9 others in London].

L.1001.g.7.

Cf. no. **100**.

40 Kinch, John. *A funeral sermon occasioned by the death of . . . Dr. John Gale: preach'd December 31. 1721.* 1722. Printed by S. Palmer for Aaron Ward.   L.1416.g.53.

41 Leybourn, William. *The compleat surveyor: or, the whole art of surveying of land.* 5th ed. 1722. For Samuel Ballard, Aaron Ward, Tho. Woodward.   L.8774.d.6.

42 Meadows, William. *A catalogue of modern English books.* [1722.] Sold by W. Meadows.
Bound with Hayes, Richard, *Rules for the port of London: or, the water-side practice* (1722), LU shelfmark: [GL] 1722.

43 Potter, John. *Archaeologia graeca: or, the antiquities of Greece.* 2 vols. 4th ed. 1722. Printed by Sam. Palmer, for J. Knapton, R. Knaplock, J. and B. Sprint, D. Midwinter, R. Robinson,

W. Taylor, W. and J. Innys, J. Osborn, W. Mears, A. Ward, and J. Bateman. L.585.d.28.
Vol. II omits Palmer's name, and contains no known SP orns.

44 [Roche, M. de la, ed.]. *Memoirs of literature.* 8 vols. 2nd ed. 1722. Sold by R. Knaplock;
and P. Vaillant. L.266.g.19.
Palmer's orns. are in Vol. III only.

45 Schickard, Wilhelm. *Wilhelmi Schickardi horologium Ebraeum.* 1722. Typis S. Palmer:
impensis J. Walthoe, J. Knapton, [and 13 others in London]. L.1607/5534.

46 Sprat, Thomas. *The history of the Royal Society of London.* 3rd ed. 1722. For S. Chapman.
L.740.c.18.
Palmer's orns. are found in a section of Part II only.

47 Thomas à Kempis. *The Christian's pattern: or, a treatise of the imitation of Jesus Christ . . . Now
render'd into English. By George Stanhope.* 10th ed. 1722. For D. Brown, J. Sprint, B. Tooke,
[and 9 others]. C. Adams 8.72.3.
Catalogued in L under: JESUS CHRIST [De imitatione Christi. *English*]; generally ascribed
to Haemmerlein, (Thomas), à Kempis. Cf. no. **96**.

1723

48 *The ascent of the separate soul, a poem.* 1723. Printed by S. Palmer for J. Morley.
L.163.m.5.

Foxon A337.

49 Bockett, Elias. *A poem to the memory of Aquila Rose, who dy'd at Philadelphia, August the 22d,
1723.* 1723–4. Printed for the author. L.G.13782(6).
Foxon B306.

50 *A defence of the negative of the two questions propos'd by Mr. Reynolds . . . to Mr. Read.* 1723. For
S. Billingsley; and sold by J. Roberts; A. Dodd; J. Billingsley; and J. Morley. LW.12.66.5(5).

51 [Lamy, Bernard]. *Apparatus Biblicus: or, an introduction to the Holy Scriptures.* [Transl. R.
Bundy.] 1723. Printed by S. Palmer. L.1167.ee.22.

52 Lisle, Samuel. *A sermon preach'd in Croydon Chapel, on Sunday August 11th, 1723.* 1723. For
Benj. Cowse. L.694.d.6(9).

53 Psalms. *Psalmi Davidis quinquaginta priores versibus elegiacus Latine redditi . . . Interprete J. H.*
[John Hanway]. 1723. Impensis autoris, & typis S. Palmer. Prostant venales apud plerosque
omnes bibliopolas. L.1007.d.14.

54 Psalms. *The whole book of Psalms: collected into English metre, by Thomas Sternhold, John
Hopkins, and others,* [etc.]. 1723. Printed by T. Wood and S. Palmer, for the Company of
Stationers. L.3434.h.4.

1724

55 Blunt, Alexander [i.e., Bockett, Elias]. *The pattern of modesty.* 1724. For A. Moore.
L.G.13782(7).

56 [Braine, Benjamin]. *A determination of the case of Mr. Thomas Story, and Mr. James Hoskins,
relating to an affair of the Pennsylvania Company, &c.* 1724. For J. Roberts. L.C.32.l.2(9).

57 [—] *The determination,* [etc.]. 2nd ed. For T. Smith.   L.G.13782(8).

58 Bysshe, Edward. *The art of English poetry.* 7th ed. 2 vols. 1725[–24]. For A. Bettesworth, J. Osborn, F. Fayram, W. Mears, J. Pemberton, C. Rivington, J. Hooke, F. Clay, J. Batley, and E. Symon.   L.992.d.3,4.
    Palmer's orns. are in Vol. II, sheets N–O^{12}: 'A dictionary of rhymes. Printed in the year 1724'.

59 Deidier, Antoine. *Dissertatio medica de morbis venereis, cui adjungitur dissertatio medico chirurgica de tumoribus.* 1724. Typis S. Palmer, sumptibus G. & J. Innys.   L.1175.l.10.

60 G[rosvenor], B[enjamin]. *A discourse on the name Jesus.* 1724. For S. Chandler.
                                                          C.Syn.7.72.36^{14}.

61 Nepos, Cornelius. *Corn. Nepotis excellentium imperatorum vitae.* Editio novissima. 1724. Typis S. Palmer, impensis J. & B. Sprint.   L.1481.dd.5.

62 Nicholas Mavrokordatos. Περὶ καθηκόντων βίβλος . . . *Liber de officiis. Graece & Latine.* 1724. Typis Samuelis Palmer.   L.526.e.23.
    Cf. no. **86**.

63 *Novus graecorum epigrammatum & poematon delectus, cum nova versione et notis. Opera Thomae Johnson . . . In usum scholae Etonensis.* 1724. Typis S. Palmer; impensis G. & J. Innys.
                                                          L.1607/1581.

64 Ovid. *Minellius Anglicanus, sive Publii Ovidii Nasonis Metamorphoseom.* [Transl. and ed. N. Bailey]. 1724. Typis S. Palmer.
    Not seen, copies in MH, NNC, PU.

65 — *Ovid's Metamorphoses. In fifteen books. Made English by several hands . . . The second edition, with great improvements by Mr. Sewell.* 2 vols. 1724. Printed by S. Palmer, for A. Bettesworth, and E. Taylor; W. Mears; and T. Woodward.   L.1473.a.6.
    Re-issued with cancel title-page as '3rd ed.' in 1726.

66 — *P. Ovidii Nasonis Metamorphoseon libri xv. Ad fidem editionis Heinsianae accuratè emendati. Cum notis Minellianis.* 1724. Impensis Societatis Stationariorum.
    Not seen, title-page is in Ames Collection (L. Ames. 6, item 2627). Palmer's printing-house orn. (Ackers orn. **89**) is present as a vignette.

67 Patrick, Simon. *A book for beginners: or, an help to young communicants, that they may be fitted for the Holy Communion, and receive it with profit.* 18th ed. 1724. Printed by S. Palmer, for D. Browne, J. Walthoe, J. Knapton, R. Knaplock, [and 14 others in London].   L.4327.a.56.

68 *Some remarks and observations relating to the transactions in the year 1720.* 1724. For J. Roberts.
                                                         C.Syn.7.72.51^{2}.

69 Terentius Afer, Publius. *Terence's comedies made English, with his life, and some remarks at the end. By Mr. Laurence Echard, and others. Revised,* [etc.]. 1724. Printed by S. Palmer, for J. Knapton, R. Knaplock, J. & B. Sprint, [and 9 others in London].   L.11707.aa.10.

70 Vossius, Gerardus. *Ger. Jo. Vossii Elementa rhetorica, oratoriis ejusdem partitionibus accommodata,* [etc.]. 1724. Typis S. Palmer, impensis G. & J. Innys.   L.117.b.30.
    Another issue has the imprint 'Apud S. Tooke & B. Motte' (copy at L.1089.g.17).

71 [Wollaston, William]. *The religion of nature delineated.* [2nd ed.]. 1724. Re-printed by Sam. Palmer; and sold by Bernard Lintott; J. Osborn; and W. and J. Innys.   L.480.c.20.

1725

72 Chandler, Samuel. *A vindication of the Christian religion.* 1725. For Samuel Chandler.
L.224.g.1.

73 Glanvill, John. *Poems: consisting of originals and translations.* 1725. For Bernard Lintot; J. Osborn and T. Longman, and W. Bell.   C.Nn.17.45.

74 Huet, Peter. *A philosophical treatise concerning the weakness of human understanding.* 1725. For Gysbert Dommer; sold by J. MacEuen, J. Clark, and S. Chandler.   C.R.17.60.

75 Pitt, Christopher. *Vida's art of poetry, translated into English verse.* 1725. Printed by Sam. Palmer, for A. Bettesworth.   L.1213.e.30.
   Foxon P416.

76 Psalms. [Psalter in Arabic, edited by Sulaiman ibn Ya'kub al-Shami al-Salihani, usually called Salomon Negri.] [1725.] [Society for the Propagation of Christian Knowledge, London.]   L.14500.c.2.
   Cf. no. **95**.

77 Selden, John. *Opera omnia, tam edita quam inedita.* 3 vols. (in 6 tomes). 1725–26.
L.G.11149–54.
   Each volume has a different imprint. Vol. II has 'Typis S. Palmer, impensis J. Walthoe [and 21 others]. 1726.' There is no imprint in the large paper issue (copy at L.19.g.1–6).

78 Turner, William. *Troporum et figurarum rhetorices praecipuarum institutio brevis.* 1725. Typis S. Palmer; prostant venales apud S. Ballard; & J. Osborn, & T. Longman.   L.624.a.25(2).

79 Wollaston, William. *The religion of nature delineated.* [3rd ed.]. 1725. Printed by S. Palmer, sold by B. Lintott, W. and J. Innys, J. Osborn, J. Batley, and T. Longman.   L.4014.g.44.

1726

80 Bible: Latin. *Biblia sacra ex Sebastiani Castellionis interpretatione, eiusque postrema recognitione.* 4 vols. 1726–27. For J. Knapton [and 12 others in London].   L.1408.e.10–13.
   The imprints for Vols. I and IV include 'Excudebat Jacob. Bettenham.'; for Vol. III, 'Excudebat Tho. Wood.'. Both Vol. II and the later sheets of Vol. IV contain SP's orns.

81 Blanckaert, Steven. *The physical dictionary.* 7th ed. 1726. For John and Benj. Sprint, and Edw. Symon.   C.7300.d.126.

82 Demosthenes. *Δημοσθένοφς λόγοι ἐκλετοί . . . Selectae orationes. In usum studiosorum hoc modo separatim excuduntur.* 1726. Typis S. Palmer. Impensis A. Bettesworth, B. Motte, & J. Redmayne; prostant etiam apud J. Knapton, J. & B. Sprint, J. Batley, & A. Ward.
L.G.16770.
   Another issue has ' . . . prostant etiam apud J. & R. Bonwicke, J. Osborn & T. Longman, & J. Newton': L shelfmark: 11391.a.7.

83 Edwards, John. *Theologia reformata.* 1726. For T. Cox.   L.3752.f.3.
Palmer probably printed only the last six sheets, 4G to 4M.

84 Guillim, John. *The banner display'd: or, an abridgment of Guillim: being a compleat system of heraldry, in all its parts . . . by Samuel Kent.* 2 vols. 1726–28. For Thomas Cox.
L.1328.e.20,21.
Kent's abridgement in octavo, of Guillim's *A display of heraldry*, of which the 6th edition, in folio, was issued in 1724. Palmer's orns. appear in Vol. I only (1726).

85 [title in Hebrew] *Liber psalmorum, editus a Johanne Leusden.* 1726. Typis S. Palmer. [For] R. & J. Bonwicke, B. Barker, S. Ballard, & J. Batley.   L.1945.c.27.

86 Nicholas Mavrokordatos. Περὶ καθηκόντων βίβλοσ . . . *Liber de officiis.* 1726. Typis S. Palmer, impensis F. Gyles.   C. Ely d.365.
Cf. no. **62**.

87 Psalms. *The whole book of psalms,* [etc., Sternhold and Hopkins]. 1726. Printed by T. Wood and S. Palmer, for the Company of Stationers.   L.3022.h.15(3).

88 Wollaston, W. *The religion of nature delineated.* [4th ed.]. 1726. Printed by Samuel Palmer, and sold by B. Lintot, W. and J. Innys, J. Osborn and T. Longman, and J. Batley.
L.8412.d.23.

1727

89 Boulainvilliers, Henri de. *État de la France,* [etc.]. 3 vols. 1727–28. Chez T. Wood & S. Palmer.   L.1857.a.8.

90 Chandler, Samuel. *Reflections on the conduct of the modern deists,* [etc.]. 1727. For John Chandler.   L.115.e.40.

91 Fleury, Claude. *The ecclesiastical history of M. l'Abbé Fleury, with the chronology of M. Tillemont.* 5 vols. 1727–31. Printed by T. Wood, for James Crokatt.   C.7.2.48–51.
Two Palmer orns. (including Ackers orn. **3**) are in Vol. I, on A2, either borrowed by Wood, or evidence of Palmer's share in printing the preliminaries. A full set of five volumes is in ZWU.

92 *Great Britain's speediest sinking fund is a powerful maritime war, rightly manag'd and especially in the West Indies.* 1727. For J. Roberts.   LU.[GL]1727.

93 Hederich, Benjamin. *M. Benj. Hederici Lexicon manuale graecum, omnibus sui generis lexicis, quae quidem exstant.* 1727. Excudit S. Palmer; impensis J. & J. Knapton, R. Knaplock, J. & B. Sprint, D. Midwinter, W. & J. Innys, J. Osborn & T. Longman, & R. Robinson.
L.1560/1687.

94 Locke, John. *The works of John Locke, Esq;.* 3 vols. 3rd ed. 1727. For Arthur Bettesworth, John Pemberton, and Edward Symon.   C.7180. b. 1–3.
Palmer's orns. are found in Vol. II, between Ff2 and Oo4. Changes in typographical style suggest Palmer printed sheets Ff to Kkk (folio in fours).

95 [*New Testament*]. [In Arabic, edited by Salomon Negri.] [1727.] [S.P.C.K.]

L.14500.d.1.

Cf. no. **76**.

96 Thomas à Kempis. *The Christian's pattern*. [Translated by] G. Stanhope. [Anr. ed.]. 1727. Printed by S. Palmer; for D. Brown, J. Knapton, R. Knaplock, J. and B. Sprint, [and 11 others in London]. L.IX.Eng.194.

Cf. no. **47**.

1728

97 Chandler, Samuel. *A vindication of the Christian religion*. 2nd ed. 1728. For S. Chandler.

L.699.g.15(1).

One known Palmer orn., four not known.

98 Coleman, Benjamin. *Some of the glories of our lord and saviour Jesus Christ, exhibited in twenty sacramental discourses, preached at Boston in New England*. 1728. Printed by S. Palmer, for Thomas Hancock . . . at Boston in New England, and sold in London by J. Osborn and T. Longman, R. Ford, and T. Cox. C.Rel.f.1.67.

99 Glover, Richard. *A poem on Sir Isaac Newton*. 1728. L.535.i.13(1).

Different setting from its appearance in no. **101** (Pemberton).

100 Juvenal & Persius. *D. Junii Juvenalis et A. Persii Flacci Satirae. Interpretatione ac notis illustravit Ludovicus Prateus*, [etc.]. 6th ed. 1728. Typis Sam. Palmer, impensis J. & B. Sprint, R. Wilkin, D. Midwinter, A. Bettesworth, S. Ballard, W. Mears, J. Batley, B. Motte, R. Ford, A. Ward, & J. Lacy. L.011388.bb.17.

Cf. no. **39**.

101 Pemberton, Henry. *A view of Sir Isaac Newton's philosophy*. 1728. Printed by S. Palmer.

L.535.i.13(1).

Another issue has: Printed by S. Palmer, for W. & J. Innys, T. Woodward, B. Lintott, C. King, T. Cox, E. Symon, A. Ward, J. Osborne, T. Longman, T. Osborne, J. Gray and J. Brindley (these are items N132 and N132.1 in Peter and Ruth Wallis, *Newton and Newtoniana 1672–1975*).

102 Wing, Vincent. *An almanack for the year of our Lord God 1728*. 1728. Printed by Samuel Palmer, for the Company of Stationers. L.N.Tab.2007/17.ᐧ

1729

103 Blunt, Alexander [i.e., Bockett, E.]. *Geneva: a poem*. 1729. For T. Payne; and sold by the booksellers of London and Westminster. L.161.k.7.

Foxon B304.

104 Clutton, Joseph. *A short and certain method of curing continu'd fevers*. 1729. Printed by S. Palmer and J. Huggonson, and sold by T. Payne, and the booksellers of London and Westminster. L.1168.k.5.

105 *The free Briton.* 'By Francis Walsingham' [William Arnall]. [Weekly journal of one, two, or (rarely) three leaves.] Nos. 1–294, 4 December 1729 to 26 June 1735. For J. Peele.

L.C.127.k.2.

After Palmer's death, continued to be printed with John Huggonson's orns.

106 Milner, John. *A practical grammar of the Latin tongue.* 1729. For John Gray.

O.Vet. A4 e. 2394(2).

107 [Mottley, John]. *The craftsman, or weekly journalist, a farce,* [etc.]. 2nd ed. 1729. For J. Roberts.

L.80.c.23(4).

108 Nepos, C. Corn. *Nepotis excellentium imperatorum vitae. Editio novissima. Cui accessit index Boecleri locupletissimus.* 1729. Impensis B. Sprint.

Not seen, title-page in Ames Collection (L. Ames. 6, item 2735).

109 Nourse, Edward. *Syllabus totam rem anatomicam humanam complectens, et praelectionibus aptatus annuatim habendis.* 1729. Typis S. Palmer & J. Huggonson. L.548.i.10(4).

110 Ovid. *P. Ovidii Nasonis Tristium libri quinque; una cum argumentis notisque Johannis Minelli . . . Opera & studio N. Bailey.* Impensis Jer. Batley; & T. Cox. O.Vet. A4 f. 1830(1).

111 Salignac de la Mothe Fénelon, François de. *Twenty-seven moral tales and fables, French and English.* [Translated by D. Bellamy.] 1729. For J. Wilcox; W. Meadows; T. Worral; A. Vandenhoeck; and J. Jackson.

L.88.b.4.

1730

112 Bedford, Arthur. *The scripture chronology demonstrated by astronomical calculations,* [etc.]. 1730. For James and John Knapton, [and 11 others in London]. O.P 3. 14 Th.

113 Blunt, Alexander [i.e., Bockett, E.]. *Blunt to Walpole: a familiar epistle in behalf of the British distillery.* 1730. For J. Wilford; and E. Bocket. L.11631.e.6. Foxon B310.

114 Boethius. *Anicius Manlius Torquatus Severinus Boetius his consolation of philosophy, in five books translated into English* [by William Causton]. 1730. Printed for the author.

ZAP.RBR.1730c.Boet.

115 Croft, R. *Remarks on the proceedings of the French court,* [etc.]. 1730. Printed by S. Palmer and J. Huggonson: and sold by J. Wilford. L.114.k.34.

116 Denne, John. *The wisdom of God in the vegetable creation. A sermon,* [etc.]. 1730. For R. Knaplock. L.225.f.9(7).

117 *The Grub-street journal.* Nos. 1–418. 8 January 1730 to 29 December 1737.

L. N. R. Burney.

Various imprints, but orns. indicate that for 1731–32 printed by Palmer and Huggonson, up to Palmer's death in May 1732, thereafter mainly by Huggonson (nos. 142, 21 Sept. 1732 to 149, 6 Nov. 1732, were 'Printed by P. Sanders, sold by Capt. Gilliver').

118 Haywood, Eliza. *Love-letters on all occasions lately passed between persons of distinction.* 1730. Printed for and sold by John Brindley; Robert Willock; John Jackson; John Penn; Francis Cogan. C.7720.d.1514.

119 *A letter to Sir William Strickland, Bart. relating to the coal trade.* 1730. Printed by S. Palmer and J. Huggonson, sold by J. Wilford.

Not seen, but copy in PU. Advertised in *Grub-street journal*, no. 11, 17 March 1730. [M., R. *The truth of the Christian faith asserted.* 1730. Printed by J. Huggonson. And sold by J. Roberts. L.4151.aaa.28.]

120 Ovid. *P. Ovidii Nasonis Metamorphosis, ex accuratissimis virorum doctissimorum castigationibus emendata, & in lucem edita.* 1730. Excudebat S. Palmer, pro Societate Stationariorum. L.11355.aa.27.

Cf. no. **9**.

121 Pine, John. *The procession and ceremonies observed at the time of the installation of the Knights Companions of the most honorable military order of the Bath: upon Thursday, June 17, 1725.* 1730. Printed by S. Palmer and J. Huggonson, for John Pine, and sold by W. Innys; F. Fayram; R. Gosling; [and 7 others in London]. L.464.h.10.

122 Wing, Vincent. *An almanack for the year of our Lord God 1730.* 1730. Printed by Samuel Palmer, for the Company of Stationers. L.N.Tab.2007/17.

1731

123 Boulainvilliers, Henri de. *The life of Mahomet.* 1731. For W. Hinchliffe.

L.10605.b.21.

Advertised in the *Grub-street journal* of 10 June 1731 as printed by S. Palmer and J. Huggonson. Ackers probably contributed one half-sheet: see note for Ackers item **39A**.

124 Greenup, John. *A vindication of human liberty.* 1731. For J. Roberts. L.8465.c.30.

125 La Fond, Jean François de. *The beauties of the language of princes*, [etc.]. [1731.] Printed (by S. Palmer and J. Huggonson) for the author. L.117.b.14.

Undated, but advertised as to be published 'On Saturday' in the *Grub-street journal*, no. 79, 8 July 1731, as *The beauties of the French tongue* by Jean de la Fond. The L catalogue has estimated the date of publication as [1720?]; but the Palmer/Huggonson partnership is not recorded before 1729.

126 Ramsay, Allan. *Poems.* 2 vols. 1731. For J. Clarke; A. Millar; F. Cogan; R. Willock, and S. Palmer and J. Huggonson, printers. [Vol. II adds W. Bickerton.] L.11630.aa.4,5.

127 Ruddiman, Thomas. *The rudiments of the Latin tongue.* 6th ed. 1731.

Not seen; advertised as printed by Palmer and Huggonson, *Grub-street journal*, no. 73, 27 May 1731.

128 Wing, Vincent. *An almanack for the year of our Lord God 1731.* 1731. Printed by Samuel Palmer, for the Company of Stationers. L.1880.c.23.

129 [Wollaston, William]. *The religion of nature delineated.* 5th ed. 1731. For James and John Knapton. L.04018.i.16.

The 6th ed. of 1738 is a re-issue, with an added preface.

130 Coker, John. *A survey of Dorsetshire*. 1732. For J. Wilcox, and S. Palmer and J. Huggonson, printers. C.LL.11.40.

The C copy, like one at L (189.f.14) is large paper; the ordinary paper issue (copy at L.983.g.10) has the imprint 'For J. Wilcox'.

131 [Cooke, Thomas]. *The comedian, or philosophical enquirer*. Nos. 1–9. 1732–33. For J. Roberts. L.PP.1253.e.

After Palmer's death in May 1732, printed by J. Huggonson alone, though the 9th issue, dated 1733, has another printer's orns. The 9 parts were re-issued with a title-page and introduction as *A demonstration of the will of God by the light of nature* (1733), for F. Cogan.

132 D'Anvers, Caleb [i.e., Amhurst, Nicholas]. *The Danverian history of the affairs of Europe, for the memorable year 1731*. 1732. For J. Roberts. L.T.1599(10).

133 — *The D'Anverian history*. 2nd ed. 1732. For J. Roberts. C.Ddd.25.139[10].

134 Hartley, James. *Speculum coeleste: being an ephemeris of the celestial motions, with an almanack for . . . 1732*. Printed by S. Palmer for the Company of Stationers. L.PP.2465(12).

135 La Mottraye, Aubry de. *The voyages and travels of A. de la Motraye*. Translated from the French. 3 vols. [Another edition.] 1732. L.986.h.14–16.

SP's orns. are in Vol. III (for E. Symon, J. Newton, and J. Oswald; L. Gilliver; J. Nourse; and T. Payne) and also on the first page of text for Vol. I (apparently a re-issue from 1723).

136 Palmer, Samuel. *The general history of printing, from its first invention in the city of Mentz, to its first progress and propagation thro' the most celebrated cities in Europe*. 1732. Printed by the author. L.619.l.11.

Partly written by George Psalmanazar. The first four sections were issued at irregular intervals between April 1729 (no. 1, dated March 1729) and November 1730 (no. 4, advertised as published 'This day' in the *Grub-street journal*, no. 47, 26 November 1730), the remaining two in August 1732 (cf. R. M. Wiles, *Serial publication in England before 1750* [Cambridge, 1957], p. 279). It was re-issued in 1733 with a slightly changed title, for A. Bettesworth, C. Hitch, and C. Davis (L.619.l.12). Part of the 1729 proposals is in the Ames Collection (L. Ames. 6, item 2742), a complete copy at NNC. The projected second volume on 'The practical art of printing' never appeared; cf. J. C. Ross, letter in the *Library*, 6th ser., 9 (1987), 384–6.

137 [Reynolds, George]. *A defence of the dissertation or inquiry concerning the gospel according to Matthew*. 1732. For T. Warner. L.689.b.22(2).

138 Vida, M. H. *Marci Hieronymi Vidae Cremonensis Albae episcopi poemata quae extant omnia*. 2 vols. 1732. Impensis Lawtoni Gilliver, & Johannis Nourse. C. Yorke d.574.

Palmer's orns. are in the preliminaries for each volume and part. The text of Vol. I contains the ornaments of James Wright (see McLaverty, p. 15).

APPENDIX III

Possible Addenda:
Pyle's *Paraphrase* (1750)

ONE 'post-Ledger' book which presents special problems is:

> Pyle, Thomas. *A paraphrase with notes, on the acts of the apostles, and upon all the epistles of the New Testament.* 2 vols. 4th ed. 1750. For R. Ware, J. and P. Knapton, D. Browne, T. Longman, C. Hitch, J. Hodges, S. Austen, J. and J. Rivington, and M. Cooper.

Only Vol. I is of interest, as Vol. II contains the orns. of another printer. Vol. I collates: 8⁰: A–Gg⁸ Hh⁴. Ackers' orns. **42** and **166** appear on A5, and orn. **80★** on C3. Eight others not known to have been used by him appear, for the first or only time, on A2, A5ᵛ, A6, B3, C2ᵛ, D2, D8ᵛ and I6ᵛ respectively. The re-appearance of several of them later in this volume indicates that the whole of it came from a single printing-house.

Two interpretations of the evidence are possible. It may be that Ackers printed this volume, and that the 8 cuts reproduced should be added to the corpus of those used by him. Alternatively, the volume could have been produced by some other printer, who had borrowed 3 of Ackers' cuts (or perhaps 2, if he were the true owner of orn. **80★**, and reciprocated by loaning it to Ackers for a single use on the half-title of John Gay's *The distress'd wife*, also dated 1750, item **164A** in Appendix I).

Ackers had printed Vol. I for the 3rd edition, issued in 1737 (*Ledger*, item **379**); and it would be consistent with other instances of his involvement in shared printing to have provided the same part of the book in the next edition. On the other hand, the disproportionate number of unknown orns., and the fact that not one of them has, as yet, been identified as in use by Ackers elsewhere during this decade, create the need for caution.

The reproductions are from volume one of the Bodleian Library copy (1015 e. 214).

Headpieces	Tailpieces	Factotums
1 9 × 77. On D8ᵛ.	**4** 21 × 43. On A5ᵛ.	**7** 22 × 22. On A6.
2 6 × 77. On B3.	**5** 20 × 46. On C2ᵛ.	**8** 19 × 19. On A2.
3 5 × 78. On D2.	**6** 18 × 27. On I6ᵛ.	

1 9×77

2 6×77

3 5×78

4 21×43

5 20×46

6 18×27

7 22×22

8 19×19

Index

Johnston, Samuel, *Sermon* (2nd ed.), N33
Johnston, William, bookseller, A2a, 83a, 314a
Journal of the campaign on the coast of France, A, 9; N23, 101, 103, 106, 184
Justin (Marcus Junius Justinus), *Ex Trogi Pompeii historiis externis*, A235
Juvenal (Decimus Junius Juvenalis), *Satirae*, with those of Persius, interpreted by Ludovicus Prateus (1722 ed.), P39; (6th ed.), N26; P100

Kennett, White, Bishop of Peterborough, A316a
Kent, Samuel, P84
Kimber, Isaac, *The history of England*, N150★
Kinch, John, *A funeral sermon*, N159; P40
King, Charles, bookseller, P101
King, R., bookseller, P25
King, William, *Ode to Myra*, N24★, 30★, 200★
Knaplock, Robert, bookseller, A21; P38, 43, 44, 67, 69, 93, 96, 116
Knapton, James, bookseller, 87; P30, 43, 45, 80, 93, 112, 129
Knapton, John, bookseller, 87; A2a, 436, 436a; P67, 69, 82, 93, 96, 112, 129
Knapton, Paul, bookseller, A2a, 436

Labelye, Charles, *The result of a view of the north level of the fens*, A241a
Lacy, James, bookseller, P100
Ladies advocate, The, A241b
La Fond, Jean François de, *The beauties of the language of princes*, P125
La Mottraye, Aubry de, *The voyages and travels*, N84, 128; P135
Lamy, Bernard, *Apparatus Biblicus*, translated by Richard Bundy, N89, 129; P51
Lancaster, N., *Sermon*, N99
Langham, Thomas, *The nett duties and drawbacks* (8th ed.), A241c
Law, Bedwell, bookseller, A37a
Laws of the Musical Society at the Castle-Tavern in Paternoster-row, The, A312
Lefèvre, Tannequi, the elder, *see* Philipps, Jenkin Thomas
Letter to Mr. Tong [et al.], A, attributed to Samuel Saunders, P18
Letter to Sir William Strickland, A, P119
Letter to William Pulteney, Esq., A, N93★
Leusden, Jan, P85
Leybourn, William, *The compleat surveyor* (5th ed.), N3, 132★, 136; P41
Life of Mr. Woolston, The, N17
Lintot, Bernard, bookseller, P23, 33, 71, 73, 79, 88, 101
Lintot, Henry, bookseller, A354, 355
Lisle, Samuel, *Sermon*, N86, 128; P52

Locke, John, *Works of* (3rd ed.), P94
Locke, Richard, *The circle squared*, A253a; *A new problem to discover the longitude at sea*, A254a
Lockman, John, *A new history of England* (2nd ed.), N33; A255
Lommius, Jodocus, *A treatise of continual fevers*, N20
London courant, The, N158
London magazine, The, 2–4, 6–7; A78c, 365a; copy with original wrapper, A270; general index (1760), N103, 117; ornaments in (in use by Ackers), 4, 6–7, 9–11; N1, 4, 5, 6, 9, 10, 14, 51, 52, 64, 87, 90, 112, 204★; use of Ackers' ornaments in, following his death, N4, 9, 51, 103, 117, 145, 162, 168, 173, 183, 184
Long, C., bookseller, A241b
Longman, Thomas (I), bookseller, 87; A2a, 297, 419a, 436, 436a; P73, 78, 79, 82, 88, 93, 98, 101
Longman, Thomas (II), bookseller, nephew of Thomas (I), A436a
Loss of liberty, The, attributed to M. Lonsdale, N7; A285
Love, John, and Ruddiman, Thomas, *Two grammatical treatises*, N16
Lownd(e)s, Thomas, bookseller, A441a
Lyttleton, George, *The progress of love*, A288

M., R., *The truth of the Christian faith*, P119+
McEuen, James, bookseller, P74
McKenzie, Donald Francis, 1, 59; co-editor of *The ledger of Charles Ackers*, 1, 59
McLaverty, J., *Pope's printer: John Wright*, ix, 1; A288; P138; *see also* Wright, John
Madness: a poem, A288a
Man and woman, A289a
Manby, Richard, bookseller, A144
Mann, Nicholas, *Of the true years of the birth and of the death of Christ*, A290
Markland, Jeremiah, classicist, A39b
Marlborough, Duke of, *see* Churchill, John
Marsh, William, printer, N167
Marshall, John, bookseller, A37a; P24
Martyn, Benjamin, *Reasons for establishing the colony of Georgia* (2nd ed.), N211
Martyn, John, editor, A346
Maslen, K. I. D., A241a, 376a; *The Bowyer ornament stock,* ix, 1, 6
Masters, Mary, *Poems on several occasions*, N176
Mather, William, *The young man's companion* (17th ed.), A297
Matthews, Emmanuel, bookseller, P14, 15, 19
Meadows, William, bookseller, *Catalogue,* P42; imprints bearing his name, A78b, 78c, 216, 218a–c, 241c, 346, 353a, 354, 355, 365a, 407, 420a, 423a; P111
Mears, William, bookseller, P43, 58, 65, 100

Sallust (Caius Sallustius Crispus), *Bellum Catilinarium*, ed. Joseph Wass, with John Minellius's notes (2nd ed.), A390

Salomon Negri, editor, P76, 95

Sanders, P., printer, P117

Saunders, Samuel, *A letter to Mr. Tong*, [*et al.*], (2nd ed.), P18

Saurin, Jacques, *Discours historiques*, N89

Say, Edward, printer, 8, 10, 56; N33, 172, 178

Schickard, Wilhelm, *Horologium Ebraeum*, P45

Scott, J., bookseller(?), A154a

'Scriblerus Quartus' [Thomas Cooke], *The bays miscellany*, N57, 67, 76, 81

Sedgwick, John, *Case*, A391a; *A short letter*, A396

Selden, John, *Opera omnia*, N86; P77

Serious and compassionate address, A, see Morris, Joseph

Sewell, George, translator, P65

Shadwell, Thomas, *Dramatick works*, N22, 180

Shakespeare, William, *Works* (Vol. VIII), N76

Sheffield, John, Duke of Buckinghamshire, *Works*, N87, 91; P31

Shelley, George, *Sentences and maxims* (3rd ed.), A395a

Shewell, Thomas, bookseller, A297

Shirley, J., bookseller (?), A253a

Short and pithy sermon against slavery, A, N161

Short letter to the letter-writer, A, A396

Simpson, Percy, *Proof-reading*, A420

Simpson, Thomas, *Elements of plane geometry*, N16

Slade, John, *Love and duty*, A400a

Smith, J., bookseller, P34

Smith, T., bookseller, P57

Society for the Propagation of Christian Knowledge (S.P.C.K.), P76, 95

Some considerations offered to the House of Commons, N177

Some objections offered to the House of Commons, N109

Some remarks and observations, P68

Some useful and occasional remarks on a libel, N76

Southern, Thomas, *Works*, N179★

Sprat, Thomas, *The history of the Royal Society* (3rd ed.), N83; P46

Sprint, Benjamin and John, booksellers, P5, 27, 38, 39, 43, 47, 61, 69, 81, 82, 93, 96, 100; (Benjamin only) 108

Stackhouse, Thomas, *A complete body of divinity* (1st ed.), N7; (2nd ed.), N2★, 113★

Stagg, John, bookseller, A225a, 316a

Stanhope, George, *see* Thomas à Kempis

Stanislaus I, The history of, A405

Stationers' Company, books printed for its English stock, 7; A177, 179, 373a, 376a; P54, 87, 102, 122, 128, 134; books printed for its Latin stock, A324a, 390; P9, 16, 66, 120

Stephens, William, *A journal of the proceedings in Georgia*, A406; *A journal received February 4, 1741*, A407; *A state of the province of Georgia*, A408

Sternhold, Thomas, *see Psalms*

Stirling, John, schoolmaster, A337a, 337b

Stone, John, bookseller, P25

Stretzer, Thomas, *The natural history of the arbor vitae*, A409

Sulaiman ibn Ya'kub al-Shami al-Salihani, *see* Salomon Negri

Swift, Jonathan, *On poetry*, N127

Switzer, Stephen, *The practical husbandman*, A411; *An universal system of water-works*, N28

Symon, Edward, bookseller, P58, 81, 94, 101, 135

Tatersal, Robert, *The bricklayer's miscellany, 2nd part*, 9; N93★

Taylor, E., bookseller, P65

Taylor, William, bookseller, P37, 43

Terence (Publius Terentius Afer), *Terence's comedies*, translated by Laurence Echard *et al.*, P69

Thomas à Kempis (i.e., Thomas Haemmerlein, à Kempis), *The Christian's pattern* [*De imitatione Christi*, attributed to him], translated by George Stanhope (10th ed.), P47; (11th ed.), N22, 27, 158; P96

Thomson, George, *The anatomy of human bones*, N31; A415

Tibullus, Albius, in *Electa majora*, A144

Tonson, Jacob (II) and Richard, booksellers, A2a

Tooke, Benjamin, bookseller, P39, 47

Tooke, S., bookseller, P70

Townsend, John, printer, ex-apprentice of Ackers, 9; Ackers' ornaments used by him, N23, 101, 103, 106, 184

Trail(e), Robert, *A steadfast adherence*, N35, 44, 82, 85, 90, 99; P12

Trapp, Joseph, *Abra-Mule*, N50; *see also* Virgil

True relation of proceedings at Salters-Hall, A, P19

Tull, Jethro, *The horse-hoing husbandry*, A417

Turner, William, *Exercises to the accidence* (8th ed.), A419a; *Troporum et figurarum rhetorices*, P78

Twells, Leonard, ed., *The theological works of Dr. Edward Pocock*, A420

Underhill, Edward, *Celsus triumphatus*, A420a

Unembarassed countenance, The, N97

Universal pocket companion, The, A421

Uvedale, Thomas, *A cure for love* (2nd ed.), A421a

Vaillant, Paul, bookseller, P44

Vallensius, Jacob, *Bibliotheca Vallensiana*, A421b

Vandenhoeck, Abraham, A421b; *Catalogus librorum*, A421c; imprint bearing his name, P111

Vida, Marcus Hieronymus, *Poemata* (1730), N105; (1732), N44, 109, 180; P138; *see also* Pitt, Christopher

View of the depredations by the Spaniards, A, A422a

Virgil (Publius Virgilius Maro), *Works, translated into English verse by Joseph Trapp* (4th ed.), A423a

Vossius, Gerardus, *Elementa rhetorica*, N29, 177; P70

W., T., (i.e., Thomas Wood?), A231

Walker, Robert, printer, 8, 10, 56; N19, 28, 37★, 43, 57, 67, 76, 81, 92, 109, 116, 161, 180

Wallis, Peter John and Ruth, *Biobibliography of British mathematics, part 2, 1701–1760*, ix; A21, 210, 216, 218a–c, 225a, 253a, 365a; P22; *Newton and Newtoniana*, A21; P101

Walpole, Sir Robert, *see Bob-lynn* (N42) *and* Musgrave, William

'Walsingham, Francis', *see Free Briton, The*

Walthoe, John, bookseller, P31, 45, 67, 77

Warburton, John, *London and Middlesex illustrated*, 8; N18; *Vallum romanum*, 8; A425

Ward, Aaron, bookseller, P38, 40, 41, 43, 82, 100, 101

Ward, John, bookseller, A2a

Ware, Richard, bookseller, 87; A2a, 14, 16a, 39, 84/95a, 99, 110, 111, 130a, 136, 137, 140, 141, 207, 297, 335, 354, 355, 436, 436a

Warner, Thomas, bookseller, A388a, 421a; P137

Wase, Christopher, *Methodi practicae specimen* (16th ed.), A431

Watts, Isaac, *The psalms of David imitated* (2nd ed.), P20

Watts, John, printer, 3; N22, 39★, 46★, 50, 83, 108, 173, 179★, 180

Ways for suppressing beggary, N28

Weekly register, The, 2–4, 6; N165–67

Welsted, Leonard, *A prologue to the town*, N127

Whiston, George, John, William, and William junior, A310a

Whitridge, Henry, bookseller, A225a

Whitworth, John, bookseller in Manchester, P10

Whole book of psalms, The (Sternhold & Hopkins), 7; A373a, 376a; P54, 87

Whole of the proceedings between Catherine and Edward Weld, The, N20, 38

Wicksteed, Edward, bookseller, A2a

Wilcox, John, bookseller, P111, 130

Wild, —, translator of *Al-Mesra*, A241

Wiles, Roy McKeen, *Serial publication in England before 1750*, P136

Wilford, John, bookseller, A26, 241; P113, 115, 119

Wilkin, R., bookseller, P39, 100

Wilkins, William, printer, N54

Willock, Robert, bookseller, A346; P118, 126

Wing, Vincent, *An almanack for 1728*, P102; *for 1730*, P122; *for 1731*, P128

Winslow, Jacobus Benignus, *An anatomical exposition, translated by George Douglas* (2nd ed.), A436; (4th ed.), A436a

Wollaston, William, *The religion of nature delineated* (2nd ed.), N128; P71; (3rd ed.), N127; P79; (4th ed.), N127, 128; P88; (5th ed.), N82, 89, 197; P129; (6th ed.), P129

Wood, John, bookseller, A144

Wood, Thomas, printer, A231; P54, 80, 87, 89, 91

Woodfall, Henry, printer, 8; N20, 24★, 33, 104★, 148; A10, 78b

Woodhead, Abraham, *Ancient church government*, ed. Simon Berington, A35

Woodman, James, bookseller, P25

Woodward, Thomas, bookseller, P41, 65, 101

Worrall, Thomas, bookseller, A78c, 225a, 365a; P111

Wright, John, printer, N70, 72, 81, 103, 107, 157; A288; P138

Yea and nay stock-jobbers, The, N141; P29

Young, Edward, *The instalment*, N8★; *The revenge: a tragedy* (another edition), A441a